The Confederate Constitution

By Sean Kevin Gravel

Table of Contents

The Confederate Constitution

The Confederate Constitution

Introduction

When the first seven Southern States seceded from the Union in 1860-1861 and formed the Confederate States of America they needed a constitution. First they produced a Provisional Constitution which was to be in effect for one year. During that time the Confederates wrote and adopted the permanent Constitution of the Confederate States of America.

The Confederate Constitution was a plagiarized version of the United States Constitution. However, there were several key differences between the two documents. Some of the changes the Confederate Founders made reflected the Confederacy's more States' Rights friendly character. Other changes provided greater and more explicit protections of slavery than the United States Constitution at the time provided.

The purpose of this book is to go line-by-line of the Confederate Constitution, comparing it with the Union Constitution as well as other important documents from American history and elaborating on the origin of its provisions and how they likely would have been applied had the Confederacy survived the Civil War. To a large extent this book will also serve as a history of the United States Constitution given the similarities between the two Constitutions. For provisions that are identical to the U.S. Constitution citations will be made to sources describing both the origin of that provision as well as case law from the

U.S. Supreme Court interpreting the meaning of those provisions. Where the two Constitutions differ I will provide the historical background likely responsible for that change as well as an explanation of how that change would likely impact Confederate society.

Note on Sources and Dedication:

The text of the Confederate Constitution appears in bold and in block quotes with deviations from the U.S. Constitution in italics. The Union version of each section is reproduced in un-bolded block quotes below the Confederate version. For the purposes of this book only the text of the Confederate Constitution as it stood in 1865 will be used. I will not speculate as to what amendments might have been added to the Confederate Constitution had the Confederacy won its independence.

The Federalist Papers were retrieved from *The Federalist Papers: Alexander Hamilton, James Madison, and John Jay*, Bantam Classic: New York, NY 1982. The Anti-Federalist Papers and debates from the Philadelphia Convention were retrieved from Ralph Ketchum, *The Anti-Federalist Papers and the Constitutional Convention Debates: The Clashes and Compromises that Gave Birth to our Form of Government*, Signet Classic: New York, NY 1986. Many of the other historical documents cited herein were retrieved from Melvin I. Urofsky and Paul Finkelman, *Documents of America Constitutional & Legal History,*

Volume I: From the Founding to 1896, 3d Ed., Oxford University Press: New York, NY 2008.

In addition to the sources cited in this book much of the historical background contained herein was learned from lectures by my various professors from both my undergraduate courses at the University of West Florida and my law school courses at Florida State University College of Law. I wish to thank them for imparting their knowledge to me. Most prominently from UWF were Professors Jocelyn Evans (professor of American Politics), William Steve Belko (professor of U.S. Constitutional and Legal History), and James Miklovich (professor of English Constitutional and Legal History) and most prominently from FSU were Professors James Gardner and Franita Tolson (professors of Constitutional Law).

Preamble

We, the people of the *Confederate* States, *each State acting in its sovereign and independent character*, in order to form *a permanent federal government*, establish justice, insure domestic tranquility, and secure the blessings of liberty to ourselves and our posterity *invoking the favor and guidance of Almighty God* do ordain and establish this Constitution for the *Confederate* States of America.

We the People of the United States, in Order to form a more perfect Union, establish Justice, insure domestic Tranquility, provide for the common defence, promote the general Welfare, and secure the Blessings of Liberty to ourselves and our Posterity, do ordain and establish this Constitution for the United States of America.

As odd as it may seem to a modern American, the opening line of the U.S. Constitution, "We the People of the United States," was very controversial when the Constitution was first proposed. The Articles of Confederation, the Union's first constitution, merely referenced the agreement between the thirteen States.[1] During Virginia's ratification convention Patrick Henry condemned the Constitution's new terminology:

> Have they made a proposal of a compact between the States? If they had, this would be a confederation: it is otherwise most clearly a consolidated government...the expression, *We, the people*, instead of the States of America.[2]

---

[1] Articles of Confederation of 1781, preamble.

[2] Speeches of Patrick Henry (June 5, 1788).

The Confederate Constitution

Anti-Federalists such as Henry believed that the United States was an association, or as the Articles of Confederates put it a "league of friendship,"[3] of semi-independent nations, not a single country, and that the proposed Constitution would strip the States of their sovereignty and independence.[4] They saw the States as the true guarantors of liberty and that a Union between them is only created by them.[5]

James Maddison rebuked this interpretation, explaining that in this case the word "People" referred to a plural form, as in thirteen groups of people.[6] In support of this reading is the First Draft of the U.S. Constitution which read, "We the people of the States of [list of the original thirteen States]."[7] The likely reason for changing the list of the thirteen States to "United States" is that the Framers were unsure of whether or not all thirteen States would ratify the Constitution and as Article VII explained only States that ratified the Constitution were part of the

---

[3] Articles of Confederation of 1781, art. III.

[4] Patrick Henry, June 5, 1788.

[5] *Id.*

[6] James Madison, as quoted in Jefferson Davis, *The Rise and Fall of the Confederation Government, Vol. 1*, 85, 112 (1881), citing Elliot's *Debates* (Washington edition, 1836), Vol. III, pages 114-15.

[7] First draft U.S.CONST., preamble, August 6, 1787.

Union. It is also noteworthy that the Treaty of Paris of 1783, the treaty ending the

Revolution, stated,

> His Brittanic Majesty acknowledges the said United
> States, viz., New Hampshire, Massachusetts Bay, Rhode
> Island and Providence Plantations, Connecticut, New
> York, New Jersey, Pennsylvania, Maryland, Virginia,
> North Carolina, South Carolina and Georgia, to be free
> sovereign and independent states.[8]

In other words, the King George III of Great Britain recognized all thirteen States

as independent countries. The use of the term "State" indicates that each State was

a sovereign nation on par with the various "States" of Europe such as Great Britain

and France, not a subdivision of a nation such as Yorkshire or Normandy.[9] The

Declaration of Independence itself reads, "these united Colonies are…Free and

Independent States…all political connection between them and the State of Great

Britain, is and ought to be totally dissolved."[10]

However, Madison also acknowledged that the Constitution created by the

Philadelphia Convention produced a hybrid between a truly federated government

---

[8] The Definitive Treaty of Peace, 1783.

[9] Kevin R.C. Gutzman, *The Politically Incorrect Guide to the Constitution*, Regnery Publishing, Inc.: Washington, D.C., 2007, 10-11.

[10] THE DECLARATION OF INDEPENDENCE para. 32 (U.S. 1776).

and a unitary government.[11] Alexander Hamilton referred to this hybrid as a "Confederate Republic."[12]

Despite this interpretation by James Madison, Chief Justice John Marshall opted for the nationalistic approach in *M'Culloch v. Maryland*.[13] Marshall rejected the argument that, "[t]he powers of the general government…are delegated by the states"[14] because, "the instrument was submitted to the *people*…the government proceeds directly from the people…The American people have declared their constitution…"[15]

The Confederate Framers rejected John Marshall's reading of the Preamble by inserting the phrase, "each State acting in its sovereign and independent character" following, "We, the people of the Confederate States." This makes it more explicit that in a truly federal form of government the people go to the States and the States go to the federal government. This statement also calls to memory the Articles of Confederation which stated that, "Each state retains its sovereignty,

---

[11] THE FEDERALIST NO. 39 (James Madison).

[12] THE FEDERALIST NO. 9 (Alexander Hamilton).

[13] 17 U.S. 316 (1819).

[14] This argument was asserted by Luther Martin, a Framer of the U.S. Constitution who represented *Maryland* in *M'Culoch v. Maryland* but lost.

[15] *Id.* at 403, 432.

freedom, and independence."[16] Chief Justice Marshall himself acknowledged that when the people act, "they act in their states."[17]

The name Confederate States of America likely originated from the United States' first constitution, the Articles of Confederation. Also, prior to the Civil War many people, foreign nations, and even the Articles of Confederation themselves referred to the United States as a "confederation" or a "confederacy." For example, Florida's Ordinance of Secession read, "the State of Florida hereby withdraws herself from the confederacy of States existing under the name of the United States of America."[18]

The second major change in the Preamble is, "in Order to form a more perfect Union" became, "in order to form a permanent federal government." The phrase "form a permanent federal government" was obviously a reference to this Constitution being the permanent Constitution proposed to replace the Confederacy's Provisional Constitution.

---

[16] Articles of Confederation of 1781, art. II.

[17] 17 U.S. 316, 403.

[18] Florida's Ordinance of Secession (January 10, 1861), https://web.archive.org/web/20040404171724/http://members.aol.com/jfepperson/ordnces.html (accessed April 16, 2018).

The Confederate Constitution

At the conclusion of the Revolution Americans debated whether or not the original thirteen States should stay in a Union together.[19] Some people considered the possibility of breaking the United States up into two or three stronger confederations, possibly along a North-South line, a move condemned by the Federalists.[20][21]

Ultimately the Framers of the Union Constitution opted to keep all thirteen States together.[22] However, less than ninety years later the Southern secessionists decided that breaking the Union up into smaller confederacies more representative of local interests was the better option. While the Southern secessionists primarily had the protection of slavery in mind,[23] many abolitionists also favored Northern secession to avoid being partnered with slavery.[24] This separation ultimately led to

---

[19] Forrest McDonald, *Novus Ordo Seclorum: The Intellectual Origins of the Constitution*, University Press of Kansas: Lawrence, KA 1985, 1.

[20] The Federalist No. 1 (Alexander Hamilton) and 2-5 (John Jay).

[21] While some Framers may have genuinely considered this, it is also quite possible that this was a straw man argument utilized by the Federalists.

[22] McDonald, *Novus Ordo Seclorum*, 185.

[23] Declaration of Causes of Seceding States, https://web.archive.org/web/19980128034930/http://sunsite.utk.edu/civil-war/reasons.html (accessed April 3, 2018); Florida Draft Declaration of Causes, http://www.civilwarcauses.org/florida-dec.htm (accessed April 3, 2018).

[24] Gutzman, *The Politically Incorrect Guide to the Constitution*, 122.

the "War between the States" that Alexander Hamilton predicted would happen under the Articles of Confederation[25] and to disastrous results for the South.

Northern and Southern politicians took differing interpretations of the phrase, "form a more perfect Union." In his inaugural address Lincoln argued that because the Articles of Confederation created a "Perpetual Union" and the Constitution made that Union "more perfect," States did not have a legal right to secede.[26] Jefferson Davis countered in his memoirs that a "more perfect Union" is one held together by fraternity and consent, not the point of a sword, meaning that secession was legal even if not preferable.[27] One Anti-Federalist feared that this phrase was actually meant to be a union of the people, not the States, and that the Constitution would be interpreted by the courts to lead to the abolition of the State governments.[28]

Historian and attorney Kevin R.C. Gutzman rebutted Lincoln's reference to the Articles of Confederation by pointing out that in the 1700s many treaties were purported to be "perpetual" which meant that there was no built-in sunset

---

[25] THE FEDERALIST NO. 8 (Alexander Hamilton).

[26] Abraham Lincoln, First Inaugural Address, (March 4, 1861). http://avalon.law.yale.edu/19th_century/ lincoln1.asp (accessed March 2, 2013).

[27] Davis, *The Rise and Fall of the Confederate Government, Vol. 1*, 145, 156-57.

[28] Brutus II Part I, February 7, 1788.

provision.[29] In other words there was no planned termination date therefore the Union was to last until further notice. Benjamin Franklin's own proposed early plan for confederation provided in Article XIII that the union of the Colonies was to be perpetual until the conflict with Great Britain was resolved.[30] The Treaty of Paris declared that a "perpetual peace" would exist between Great Britain and the United States,[31] but the War of 1812 proved that "perpetual" does not mean "forever."

Of the delegates to the Philadelphia Convention Gouvernor Morris stated that it was perfectly constitutional for a State to secede from the Union under certain circumstances[32] while James Maddison said that secession was unconstitutional.[33] Andrew Jackson once argued that if territories were subject to Congressional regulation it was illogical that they could gain the right to secede by becoming States. The counter to that argument is that when new States are

---

[29] Gutzman, *The Politically Incorrect Guide to the Constitution*, 12, 96.

[30] Benjamin Franklin, Benjamin Franklin's Articles of Confederation, May 10 1775, retrieved from http://www.usconstitution.net/franklinart.html (accessed September 10, 2017).

[31] The Definitive Treaty of Peace, 1783.

[32] McDonald, *Novus Ordo Seclorum*, 281.

[33] James Maddison, Letter to Edward Everett, August 28, 1830. http://www.constitutionreader.com/reader.engz?doc=constitution&chapter=OEBP S/Text/ch78.xhtml (accessed June 12, 2018).

admitted to the Union they are admitted on equal footing with the original States.[34] In the months leading up to the Civil War Representative Otis S. Ferry of Connecticut proposed a constitutional amendment to prohibit secession without the consent of Congress and the President, implicitly recognizing that such a right existed.[35] Perhaps the British military historian Colonel G.F.R. Henderson stated it best when he noted that secession did not go against the letter of the Constitution, but perhaps it went against the spirit of it.[36] The Supreme Court (benched by five Lincoln appointees) in a five to three vote sided with Lincoln and Maddison in *Texas v. White*, ruling that, "the Constitution…looks to an indestructible Union, composed of indestructible States."[37]

The Confederates eliminated the objectives to, "provide for the common defence, promote the general Welfare." Since federal governments are governments of limited powers that can only exercise powers delegated by their creating documents, this change was presumably made to reduce claims of implied powers, a doctrine laid down in the *M'Culloch* decision stating that Congress has

---

[34] Gutzman, *The Politically Incorrect Guide to the Constitution*, 21.

[35] *Id.* at 122-23.

[36] G.F.R. Henderson, *The Civil War: A Soldier's View*, The University of Chicago Press, Chicago, IL, 1958, 175.

[37] 74 U.S. 700, 726 (1868).

powers beyond those expressly delegated.[38] James Maddison commented that if the people of Virginia had foreseen the implied powers doctrine the Virginia Ratifying Convention would have rejected the U.S. Constitution.[39]

The final change to the Preamble is an invocation of God. This addressed one minor Anti-Federalist criticism to the Constitution: that it made no explicit reference to God other than in the date ("in the year of our Lord") and excepting Sundays from days the President has to consider a bill.[40] The Declaration of Independence by contrast referenced, "the Laws of Nature and of Nature's God"[41] and the Articles of Confederation referenced, "the Great Governor of the World."[42]

In the past century many people used the First Amendment to the United States Constitution to challenge references to God in public forums such as the phrase "under God" in the Pledge of Allegiance or the motto "In God we Trust" on currency. While the Confederate Constitution has an equivalent to the First Amendment (discussed later), this clause in the Preamble would certainly foreclose lawsuits against generic references to God in government settings. It should also

---

[38] *Id.* at 406.

[39] Gutzman, *The Politically Incorrect Guide to the Constitution*, 83, 93-94.

[40] U.S. CONST. art. I section 7.

[41] THE DECLARATION OF INDEPENDENCE para. 1 (U.S. 1776).

[42] Articles of Confederation of 1781, art. XIII.

be noted that some State Constitutions make similar invocations. For example,

Florida's Preamble reads, "We, the people of the State of Florida, being grateful to

Almighty God for our constitutional liberty…do ordain and establish this

constitution."[43]

---

[43] FLA. CONST. preamble.

ARTICLE I

Section I.

All legislative powers herein *delegated* shall be vested in a Congress of the Confederate States, which shall consist of a Senate and House of Representatives.

All legislative Powers herein granted shall be vested in a Congress of the United States, which shall consist of a Senate and House of Representatives.

The word "Congress" implies an assembly of representatives or ambassadors of sovereign nations (compare to the Congresses of Westphalia and Vienne).[44]

The idea for a two-house Congress was inspired by the British Parliament which has a lower House of Commons popularly elected by qualified voters and an upper House of Lords made up of the hereditary nobility and church officials.[45] At the Philadelphia Convention Edmund Randolph proposed the Virginia Plan previously conceived by James Maddison which called for a bicameral legislature with a lower house chosen by the people and the upper house chosen by the lower house as opposed to the Articles of Confederation's unicameral legislature with members chosen by the State governments.[46] John Dickinson proposed using these

---

[44] Gutzman, *The Politically Incorrect Guide to the Constitution*, 10.

[45] Ralph Ketcham, Introduction to *The Anti-Federalist Papers and the Constitutional Convention Debates: The Clashes and the Compromises that Gave Birth to our Form of Government*, Signet Classic: New York, NY 2003, 7.

[46] Edmund Randolph, "The Virginia Plan," May 29, 1787.

two houses to create a blend between purely national and purely Federal government by having one House with members popularly elected by the people and the other with members chosen by the State Legislatures.[47] This plan was refined and eventually resulted in the Congress of the United States.

The only change in the Confederate version, other than "United" to "Confederate," is that the word "granted" became "delegated," perhaps to make it clear to the Confederate courts that the Federal government of the Confederacy was one of limited powers and that new powers were not to be read in.

Sec. 2.

(1)

> **The House of Representatives shall be composed of members chosen every second year by the people of the several States; *and the electors in each State shall be citizens of the Confederate States, and* have the qualifications requisite for electors of the most numerous branch of the State Legislature; *but no person of foreign birth, not a citizen of the Confederate States, shall be allowed to vote for any officer, civil or political, State or Federal.***

> The House of Representatives shall be composed of Members chosen every second Year by the People of the several States, and the Electors in each State shall have the Qualifications requisite for Electors of the most numerous Branch of the State Legislature.

---

[47] McDonald, *Novus Ordo Seclorum*, 215. See also THE FEDERALIST NO. 39 (James Madison).

The concept that one House should be elected by the people of the States originated with the Virginia Plan. The idea of elections every two years stemmed from the need of frequent elections to reflect the sympathies of the people.[48] However, if elections were held too frequently it might discourage worthy men from seeking election, prevent lawmakers from gaining valuable experience, and raise difficulties in challenging the validity of elections.[49]

This clause is one instance in which the Confederate Constitution actually eliminated a State right, the ability to give the right to vote to non-citizens. Originally the States had the full power to decide who could vote. The Framers of the U.S. Constitution decided to not interfere with this as the States were the best judges of their own people.[50] While later amendments to the United States Constitution prohibited States from disqualifying people from voting on certain grounds, such as race and sex, nothing in the U.S. Constitution restricts the ability of the States to extend the franchise to certain classes of people traditionally excluded, such as non-citizens or minors.

However, this new clause in the Confederate Constitution did nothing more than codify what was already a common practice. No State in the United States,

---

[48] THE FEDERALIST NO. 52 (James Maddison).

[49] THE FEDERALIST NO. 53 (James Maddison).

[50] "Qualifications for Suffrage," August 7, 1787.

then or now, extends the franchise to non-citizens for State and Federal offices, although there are movements in some States to do so at least on a local level.[51] This was eluded to in the Fourteenth Amendment to the U.S. Constitution which allowed Congress to reduce a State's representation in the House if that State denies the right to vote to any male inhabitant of the State who is at least twenty-one years old and a U.S. citizen.[52]

One possible reason for the inclusion of this clause in the Confederate Constitution was to prevent Unionists from crossing into the Confederacy, registering to vote, and then overturning the South's secession. The Framers of the U.S. Constitution had something similar in mind: they knew that recent immigrants often had attachments to the form of government of their homelands.[53] To preserve America's republicanism a naturalized foreigner had to be a citizen for seven years to be a Representative, nine years to be a Senator, and a natural born citizen with fourteen years of residency to be President.[54] Since the Confederates

---

[51] Rachel Chason, "Non-citizens can now vote in College Park, Md.," The Washington Post, September 12, 2017. https://www.washingtonpost.com/local/md-politics/college-park-decides-to-allow-noncitizens-to-vote-in-local-elections/2017/09/13/2b7adb4a-987b-11e7-87fc-c3f7ee4035c9_story.html?utm_term=.b6643b3f6bfc (accessed July 18, 2018).

[52] U.S. CONST. amendment XIV, section 2.

[53] "Citizenship for Immigrants," August 9, 1787.

[54] Id.

dispensed with those requirements for members of Congress (explained below) perhaps the added provision of requiring citizenship to vote was to balance out the elimination of those requirements.

The following Amendments to the U.S. Constitution restricted the States' right to deny the franchise to certain classes of people:

Fourteenth Amendment:

> ...when the right to vote at any election for the choice of electors for President and Vice President of the United States, Representatives in Congress, the Executive and Judicial officers of a State, or the members of the Legislature thereof, is denied to any of the male inhabitants of such State, being twenty-one years of age, and citizens of the United States, or in any way abridged, except for participation in rebellion, or other crime, the basis of representation therein shall be reduced in the proportion which the number of such male citizens shall bear to the whole number of male citizens twenty-one years of age in such State.

Fifteenth Amendment:

> The right of citizens of the United States to vote shall not be denied or abridged by the United States or by any State on account of race, color, or previous condition of servitude.

Nineteenth Amendment:

> The right of citizens of the United States to vote shall not be denied or abridged by the United States or by any State on account of sex.

Twenty-Fourth Amendment:

The right of citizens of the United States to vote in any primary or other election for President or Vice President, for electors for President or Vice President, or for Senator or Representative in Congress, shall not be denied or abridged by the United States or any state by reason of failure to pay any poll tax or other tax.

Twenty-Sixth Amendment:

The right of citizens of the United States, who are 18 years of age or older, to vote, shall not be denied or abridged by the United States or any state on account of age.

(2)

No person shall be a Representative who shall not have attained the age of twenty-five years, and be a citizen of the Confederate States, and who shall not when elected, be an inhabitant of that State in which he shall be chosen.

No Person shall be a Representative who shall not have attained to the Age of twenty five Years, and been seven Years a Citizen of the United States, and who shall not, when elected, be an Inhabitant of that State in which he shall be chosen.

The Confederate Constitution eliminated the seven year residency requirement from its Union counterpart. The obvious reason for this elimination was because at the time of the Confederate Constitution was written the Confederacy had only existed for one month. The U.S. Constitution by contrast was written eleven years after the Declaration of Independence was adopted.

(3)

Representatives and direct taxes shall be apportioned among the several States, which may be included within this Confederacy, according to their respective numbers, which shall be determined by adding to the whole number of free persons, including those bound to service for a term of years, and excluding Indians not taxed, three-fifths of all *slaves*. The actual enumeration shall be made within three years after the first meeting of the Congress of the Confederate States, and within every subsequent term of ten years, in such manner as they shall by law direct. The number of Representatives shall not exceed one for every *fifty* thousand, but each State shall have at least one Representative; and until such enumeration shall be made, *the State of South Carolina shall be entitled to choose six; the State of Georgia ten; the State of Alabama nine; the State of Florida two; the State of Mississippi seven; the State of Louisiana six; and the State of Texas six.*

Representatives and direct Taxes shall be apportioned among the several States which may be included within this Union, according to their respective Numbers, which shall be determined by adding to the whole Number of free Persons, including those bound to Service for a Term of Years, and excluding Indians not taxed, three fifths of all other Persons. The actual Enumeration shall be made within three Years after the first Meeting of the Congress of the United States, and within every subsequent Term of ten Years, in such Manner as they shall by Law direct. The Number of Representatives shall not exceed one for every thirty Thousand, but each State shall have at Least one Representative; and until such enumeration shall be made, the State of New Hampshire shall be entitled to chuse three, Massachusetts eight, Rhode-Island and Providence Plantations one, Connecticut five, New-York six, New Jersey four, Pennsylvania eight, Delaware one,

Maryland six, Virginia ten, North Carolina five, South Carolina five, and Georgia three.

The apportioning of Representatives based on State populations was a nationalistic move on the part of the Philadelphia Convention based on complaints regarding equal representation of all of the States under the Articles of Confederation. The biggest complaint was that a super-majority of States could contain a minority of the population, but that minority could coerce a majority of Americans.[55] Defenders of this rule pointed out that in a truly federal union each State is a co-equal member.[56]

The three-fifths compromise settled a dispute between whether or not slaves should be counted. At the time of the Philadelphia Convention twelve of the thirteen States allowed slavery (Massachusetts abolished it in 1781). Because Northern States had few slaves and were in the process of phasing out slavery they did not want slaves to be counted. The Southern States by contrast had large slave populations, and Northern slave holders were selling their slaves South, so they wanted the slaves counted to increase their representation. The North pointed out that slaves were treated as property. The South could respond that women and children also had limited rights yet they were still counted. Maddison

---

[55] THE FEDERALIST NO. 22 (Alexander Hamilton).

[56] Gutzman, *The Politically Incorrect Guide to the Constitution*, 13.

acknowledged that in some respects slaves were property but in other respects they were people.[57] Eventually the Framers decided that three-fifths of slaves, a percentage originally suggested in the New Jersey Plan,[58] would be counted. Some abolitionists like Frederick Douglas claimed that the North was trying to encourage the South to free its slaves with this clause, but in reality this was merely a compromise over a power struggle.

Curiously, the Confederates retained the three-fifths clause despite every Confederate State being a slave State. Maybe this reflected their belief in white supremacy, or maybe they simply did not want to interfere with the Union Framer's formula. However, they expressly referenced slaves and slavery whereas the Union Framers utilized euphemisms such as, "all other Persons." The Union Framers' use of euphemisms possibly reflects the embarrassment many of them felt regarding slavery thus lead to a policy of interpreting any ambiguity in the Constitution regarding slavery against slavery while the Confederates' unashamed references to it could lead to any ambiguity being interpreted in favor of it.

The Confederates also reduced the maximum size of the House from one representative for every 30,000 people, the number proposed by George

---

[57] THE FEDERALIST NO. 54 (James Maddison).

[58] "The New Jersey Plan," June 15, 1787.

Washington,[59] to one for every 50,000. One Anti-Federalist noted that this latter number actually resembled the arrangement of the first House of Representatives before the first census was taken.[60] However, this change is of little substance as having a House of Representatives with the maximum possible size under either Constitution would be too large and unworkable today given the population growth since 1787 and 1861.

In this regard the Confederates went against an Anti-Federalist concern by reducing the size of the House. The Anti-Federalists thought that the United States was too large, nearly 3,000,000 people at the time, to adequately represent the people and that one representative for every 30,000 people was not enough.[61] James Maddison defended the idea of a large republic, arguing that it was necessary to combat the evils generated by faction as the most worthy candidates could garner enough support to win an election.[62] Regarding the size of the House Maddison noted that a moderate line had to be drawn somewhere to balance

---

[59] Joseph J. Ellis, *His Excellency*, Alfred A. Knopf: New York, NY 2004, 177-78.

[60] Pennsylvania Minority, December 18, 1787.

[61] Patrick Henry, June 5, 1788; Brutus, October 18, 1787.

[62] THE FEDERALIST NO. 10 (James Maddison).

sufficient representation with practicality.[63] The Anti-Federalists by contrast thought that it would be easier for unworthy candidates to win in a large republic as they could resort to corruption to manipulate a large, uninformed electorate.[64] Maddison responded that the electors who chose Representatives were the same people who voted in State elections.[65]

The Confederate Constitution also lists different States as founding members and assigns them different numbers of representatives for Georgia and South Carolina to reflect the increase in population since the U.S. Constitution was written.

Subsequent amendments to the U.S. Constitution changed the implication of this subsection for the Union. Section 2 of the Fourteenth Amendment reads in part,

> Representatives shall be apportioned among the several States according to their respective numbers, counting the whole number of persons in each State, excluding Indians not taxed.

The Sixteenth Amendment reads,

> The Congress shall have power to lay and collect taxes on incomes, from whatever source derived, without

---

[63] THE FEDERALIST NO. 55-56 (James Maddison).

[64] Patrick Henry, June 5, 1788; Brutus, October 18, 1787.

[65] THE FEDERALIST NO. 57 (James Maddison.

apportionment among the several States, and without regard to any census or enumeration.

(4)

When vacancies happen in the representation from any State the executive authority thereof shall issue writs of election to fill such vacancies.

When vacancies happen in the Representation from any State, the Executive Authority thereof shall issue Writs of Election to fill such Vacancies.

(5)

The House of Representatives shall choose their Speaker and other officers; and shall have the sole power of impeachment; *except that any judicial or other Federal officer, resident and acting solely within the limits of any State, may be impeached by a vote of two-thirds of both branches of the Legislature thereof.*

The House of Representatives shall chuse their Speaker and other Officers; and shall have the sole Power of Impeachment.

This subsection of the Confederate Constitution gave States the ability to impeach Federal officers who operate exclusively within their borders. For example, Federal trial judges, prosecutors, postmasters, tax collectors, and any other official that did not have a jurisdiction that crossed State lines would be subject to impeachment by the State Legislatures.

Sec. 3.

(1) The Senate of the *Confederate* States shall be composed of two Senators from each State, chosen for six years by the Legislature thereof, *at the regular session next immediately preceding the commencement of the term of service*; and each Senator shall have one vote.

The Union version originally read,

> The Senate of the United States shall be composed of two Senators from each State, chosen by the Legislature thereof, for six Years; and each Senator shall have one Vote.

but the Section 1 of the Seventeenth Amendment altered the Union version:

> The Senate of the United States shall be composed of two Senators from each State, elected by the people thereof, for six years; and each Senator shall have one vote. The electors in each State shall have the qualifications requisite for electors of the most numerous branch of the State legislatures.

Equal representation in the Senate implied that the States were still somewhat sovereign, and as equal sovereignties they were entitled to equal representation regardless of State population.[66] The added clause to the Confederate version likely related to the Provisional Constitution, providing for continuity in government.

---

[66] THE FEDERALIST NO. 62 (James Maddison).

Many at the Philadelphia Convention argued for election of Senators by State Legislatures as the average voter lacks information on State-wide issues and could easily be misled.[67] In 1913 the United States switched to direct election of Senators, a plan favored by some but rejected in 1787.[68]

(2)

> **Immediately after they shall be assembled, in consequence of the first election, they shall be divided as equally as may be into three classes. The seats of the Senators of the first class shall be vacated at the expiration of the second year; of the second class at the expiration of the fourth year; and of the third class at the expiration of the sixth year; so that one-third may be chosen every second year; and if vacancies happen by resignation, or other wise, during the recess of the Legislature of any State, the Executive thereof may make temporary appointments until the next meeting of the Legislature, which shall then fill such vacancies.**

> Immediately after they shall be assembled in Consequence of the first Election, they shall be divided as equally as may be into three Classes. The Seats of the Senators of the first Class shall be vacated at the Expiration of the second Year, of the second Class at the Expiration of the fourth Year, and of the third Class at the Expiration of the sixth Year, so that one third may be chosen every second Year; and if Vacancies happen by Resignation, or otherwise, during the Recess of the Legislature of any State, the Executive thereof may make temporary Appointments until the next Meeting of the Legislature, which shall then fill such Vacancies.

---

[67] Roger Sherman, "Debate on Representation," May 31, 1787.

[68] James Wilson, "Debate on Method of Electing Senators," June 7, 1787.

The staggering of terms was designed to ensure continuity in government, something necessary for foreign diplomacy.[69] Section 2 of the Seventeenth Amendment changed the procedure for replacing Senators in the Union:

> When vacancies happen in the representation of any State in the Senate, the executive authority of such State shall issue writs of election to fill such vacancies: Provided, That the legislature of any State may empower the executive thereof to make temporary appointments until the people fill the vacancies by election as the legislature may direct.

(3)

> **No person shall be a Senator who shall not have attained the age of thirty years, and be a citizen of the *Confederate* States; and who shall not, then elected, be an inhabitant of the State for which he shall be chosen.**

> No Person shall be a Senator who shall not have attained to the Age of thirty Years, and been nine Years a Citizen of the United States, and who shall not, when elected, be an Inhabitant of that State for which he shall be chosen.

The Senate has more stringent requirements than the House because its responsibilities require greater knowledge and stability of character.[70] The Union had one additional requirement which the Confederacy dispensed with due to its young age.

---

[69] Garry Wills, Introduction to *The Federalist Papers*, Bantam Classics: New York, NY 2003, xviii.

[70] THE FEDERALIST NO. 62 (James Maddison).

(4)

The Vice President of the *Confederate* States shall be president of the Senate, but shall have no vote unless they be equally divided.

The Vice President of the United States shall be President of the Senate, but shall have no Vote, unless they be equally divided.

(5)

The Senate shall choose their other officers; and also a president pro tempore in the absence of the Vice President, or when he shall exercise the office of President of the *Confederate* states.

The Senate shall chuse their other Officers, and also a President pro tempore, in the Absence of the Vice President, or when he shall exercise the Office of President of the United States.

(6)

The Senate shall have the sole power to try all impeachments. When sitting for that purpose, they shall be on oath or affirmation. When the President of the *Confederate* States is tried, the Chief Justice shall preside; and no person shall be convicted without the concurrence of two-thirds of the members present.

The Senate shall have the sole Power to try all Impeachments. When sitting for that Purpose, they shall be on Oath or Affirmation. When the President of the United States is tried, the Chief Justice shall preside: And no Person shall be convicted without the Concurrence of two thirds of the Members present.

(7)

> **Judgment in cases of impeachment shall not extend further than to removal from office, and disqualification to hold any office of honor, trust, or profit under the *Confederate* States; but the party convicted shall, nevertheless, be liable and subject to indictment, trial, judgment, and punishment according to law.**

> Judgment in Cases of impeachment shall not extend further than to removal from Office, and disqualification to hold and enjoy any Office of honor, Trust or Profit under the United States: but the Party convicted shall nevertheless be liable and subject to Indictment, Trial, Judgment and Punishment, according to Law.

Sec. 4.

(1)

> **The times, places, and manner of holding elections for Senators and Representatives shall be prescribed in each State by the Legislature thereof, *subject to the provisions of this Constitution*; but the Congress may, at any time, by law, make or alter such regulations, except as to *the times* and places of choosing Senators.**

> The Times, Places and Manner of holding Elections for Senators and Representatives, shall be prescribed in each State by the Legislature thereof; but the Congress may at any time by Law make or alter such Regulations, except as to the Places of chusing Senators.

The Confederate Framers made two small additions to this section. The first related to additional limitations of the Confederate Constitution, such as the citizenship to vote requirement and the schedule provided in Article VII, Section 2. The second change restricted Congress' power to set the time for the elections, allowing the States to adopt different election days should they choose. This answered an Anti-Federalist criticism that Congress may try to circumvent elections by delaying them, allowing government officials to stay in office indefinitely.[71] Hamilton defended this clause as, "*every government ought to contain in itself the means of its own preservation*"[72] (logic later used by Lincoln to justify his various war measures). Hamilton argued that the power to regulate elections must rest somewhere, and if it rested solely in the State legislatures the existence of the Union would be entirely at their mercy.[73] The Confederates apparently were not satisfied with this answer.

(2)

> **The Congress shall assemble at least once in every year; and such meeting shall be on the first Monday in December, unless they shall, by law, appoint a different day.**
>
> The Congress shall assemble at least once in every Year, and such Meeting shall be on the first Monday in December, unless they shall by Law appoint a different Day.

---

[71] Pennsylvania Minority (December 18, 1787); Jackson Turner Maine, *The Anti-Federalists: Critics of the Constitution, 1781-1788*, The University of North Carolina Press: 1961, 150.

[72] THE FEDERALIST NO. 59 (Alexander Hamilton).

[73] *Id.*

The Section 2 of the Twentieth Amendment to the U.S. Constitution altered this:

> The Congress shall assemble at least once in every year, and such meeting shall begin at noon on the 3d day of January, unless they shall by law appoint a different day.

Sec. 5.

(1)

> **Each House shall be the judge of the elections, returns, and qualifications of its own members, and a majority of each shall constitute a quorum to do business; but a smaller number may adjourn from day to day, and may be authorized to compel the attendance of absent members, in such manner and under such penalties as each House may provide.**

> Each House shall be the Judge of the Elections, Returns and Qualifications of its own Members, and a Majority of each shall constitute a Quorum to do Business; but a smaller Number may adjourn from day to day, and may be authorized to compel the Attendance of absent Members, in such Manner, and under such Penalties as each House may provide.

(2)

> **Each House may determine the rules of its proceedings, punish its members for disorderly behavior, and, with the concurrence of two-thirds *of the whole number*, expel a member.**

> Each House may determine the Rules of its Proceedings, punish its Members for disorderly Behaviour, and, with the Concurrence of two thirds, expel a Member.

The Union Constitution presumably makes it is slightly easier for a House of Congress to expel one of its members, apparently only requiring two-thirds of those present to vote in favor of expulsion. The Confederate version required a vote of two-thirds of that House's total membership to expel a member.

(3)

> **Each House shall keep a journal of its proceedings, and from time to time publish the same, excepting such parts as may in their judgment require secrecy; and the yeas and nays of the members of either House, on any question, shall, at the desire of one-fifth of those present, be entered on the journal.**

> Each House shall keep a Journal of its Proceedings, and from time to time publish the same, excepting such Parts as may in their Judgment require Secrecy; and the Yeas and Nays of the Members of either House on any question shall, at the Desire of one fifth of those Present, be entered on the Journal.

One minor controversy that arose in the United States under this clause was the censure of Andrew Jackson for removing Federal deposits from the Second National Bank of the United States.[74] Jackson and his Democrats declared censure to be unauthorized. When the Democrats retook the Senate from the Whig Party they expunged this censure from the Senate journal, a move opposed by Whigs

---

[74] Jon Meacham, *American Lion: Andrew Jackson in the White House*, Random House: New York, NY 2008, 278-79.

such as John C. Calhoun who cited this section's requirement that each house keep a journal of its proceedings.[75]

(4)

> **Neither House, during the session of Congress, shall, without the consent of the other, adjourn for more than three days, nor to any other place than that in which the two Houses shall be sitting.**

> Neither House, during the Session of Congress, shall, without the Consent of the other, adjourn for more than three days, nor to any other Place than that in which the two Houses shall be sitting.

Sec. 6.

(1)

> **The Senators and Representatives shall receive a compensation for their services, to be ascertained by law, and paid out of the Treasury of the *Confederate* States. They shall, in all cases, except treason, felony, and breach of the peace, be privileged from arrest during their attendance at the session of their respective Houses, and in going to and returning from the same; and for any speech or debate in either House, they shall not be questioned in any other place. No Senator or Representative shall, during the time for which he was elected, be appointed to any civil office under the authority of the *Confederate* States, which shall have been created, or the emoluments whereof shall have been increased during such time; and no person holding any office under the *Confederate* States shall be a member of either House during his continuance in office. *But Congress may, by law, grant to the principal officer in each of the***

---

[75] *Id.* at 335-38.

Executive Departments a seat upon the floor of either House, with the privilege of discussing any measures appertaining to his department.

The Senators and Representatives shall receive a Compensation for their Services, to be ascertained by Law, and paid out of the Treasury of the United States. They shall in all Cases, except Treason, Felony and Breach of the Peace, be privileged from Arrest during their Attendance at the Session of their respective Houses, and in going to and returning from the same; and for any Speech or Debate in either House, they shall not be questioned in any other Place.

No Senator or Representative shall, during the Time for which he was elected, be appointed to any civil Office under the Authority of the United States, which shall have been created, or the Emoluments whereof shall have been encreased during such time; and no Person holding any Office under the United States, shall be a Member of either House during his Continuance in Office.

The clause prohibiting members of Congress from accepting other offices was a balance of power provision to reduce the ability of the President from trying to influence votes by offering patronage jobs.[76] However, the Framers left open the possibility of a member of Congress resigning to take another office in hopes that it might channel self-interested motives into productive policy.[77]

The Confederates added a clause confirming a common practice in the United States by allowing Cabinet members to speak before Congress regarding

---

[76] McDonald, *Novus Ordo Seclorum*, 199-200.

[77] *Id.* at 200.

their departments. The U.S. Constitution was subsequently amended regarding

Congressional salaries. The Twenty-Seventh Amendment to the Constitution was

proposed in 1789 with the rest of the Bill of Rights, but it was not ratified until

1992. It reads:

> No law varying the compensation for the services of the
> Senators and Representatives shall take effect until an
> election of Representatives shall have intervened.

Sec. 7.

(1)

> **All bills for raising revenue shall originate in the**
> **House of Representatives; but the Senate may**
> **propose or concur with amendments, as on other bills.**

> All Bills for raising Revenue shall originate in the House
> of Representatives; but the Senate may propose or concur
> with Amendments as on other Bills.

The requirement that money bills original in the House stems from English

procedure where money bills originate in the House of Commons.[78] This is

because taxes were seen as voluntary gifts from the people to the government

through their duly elected representatives.[79] Of course people are usually more

generous to give away other people's money, which led to many early restrictions

_____

[78] *Id.* at 26-27.

[79] *Id.* at 27.

on who could vote, such as restricting the franchise to property holders.[80] By the

Jacksonian Era most States achieved universal (i.e. white-male) suffrage.

(2)

> **Every bill which shall have passed both Houses, shall, before it becomes a law, be presented to the President of the Confederate States; if he approve, he shall sign it; but if not, he shall return it, with his objections, to that House in which it shall have originated, who shall enter the objections at large on their journal, and proceed to reconsider it. If, after such reconsideration, two-thirds of that House shall agree to pass the bill, it shall be sent, together with the objections, to the other House, by which it shall likewise be reconsidered, and if approved by two-thirds of that House, it shall become a law. But in all such cases, the votes of both Houses shall be determined by yeas and nays, and the names of the persons voting for and against the bill shall be entered on the journal of each House respective}y. If any bill shall not be returned by the President within ten days (Sundays excepted) after it shall have been presented to him, the same shall be a law, in like manner as if he had signed it, unless the Congress, by their adjournment, prevent its return; in which case it shall not be a law.** *The President may approve any appropriation and disapprove any other appropriation in the same bill. In such case he shall, in signing the bill, designate the appropriations disapproved; and shall return a copy of such appropriations, with his objections, to the House in which the bill shall have originated; and the same proceedings shall then be had as in case of other bills disapproved by the President.*

> Every Bill which shall have passed the House of Representatives and the Senate, shall, before it become a

---

[80] *Id.* at 27-28.

Law, be presented to the President of the United States; If he approve he shall sign it, but if not he shall return it, with his Objections to that House in which it shall have originated, who shall enter the Objections at large on their Journal, and proceed to reconsider it. If after such Reconsideration two thirds of that House shall agree to pass the Bill, it shall be sent, together with the Objections, to the other House, by which it shall likewise be reconsidered, and if approved by two thirds of that House, it shall become a Law. But in all such Cases the Votes of both Houses shall be determined by yeas and Nays, and the Names of the Persons voting for and against the Bill shall be entered on the Journal of each House respectively. If any Bill shall not be returned by the President within ten Days (Sundays excepted) after it shall have been presented to him, the Same shall be a Law, in like Manner as if he had signed it, unless the Congress by their Adjournment prevent its Return, in which Case it shall not be a Law.

This section in both Constitutions outlines the process by which a bill becomes law which with one exception is exactly the same in both versions. The power of the President to veto a law is a traditional check and balance the executive has had on the legislative branch, an absolute power retained by the British monarch.[81] Most American Colonies distrusted the veto power, placing limits on their governors' veto.[82] The U.S. Framers followed suit by allowing a two-third super-majority in each House of Congress to override a Presidential veto. Andrew Jackson used the veto power to claim that he was bound to uphold the

---

[81] *Id.* at 82-83, 86.

[82] *Id.* at 86.

Constitution as he understood it thus he could veto a bill as unconstitutional even if the Supreme Court previously held such a law constitutional.[83]

The Supreme Court of the United States elaborated on this clause in *I.N.S. v. Chada*, holding that a provision of the Immigration and Nationality Act that allowed a House of Congress to veto the decision of the President to not deport a deportable alien was unconstitutional as it violated the Presentment clause.[84] This one-House veto could not stand as it allowed a single House of Congress to exercise power delegated to the President.[85] The Court noted that convenience and efficiency were not hallmarks of a democratic government.[86]

The key difference between the Union and Confederate Constitutions in this section is that the Confederate President was expressly conferred a line-item veto. This allowed the President to strike budgetary appropriations by Congress, but Congress by a two-thirds vote in each house could restore each appropriation. This answered a concern of the Anti-Federalists that Congress could contract debts at its discretion and use those debts to justify increased taxation.[87]

---

[83] Andrew Jackson, Veto of Bank Bill (1832).

[84] 462 U.S. 919, 952-59 (1983).

[85] *Id.*

[86] *Id.* at 944.

[87] Brutus I and VI, October 18, 1787 and December 27, 1787.

The reasoning behind a line-item veto is that it helps promote a balanced budget. Each member of Congress, particularly in the House of Representatives where money bills originate, has to answer to a smaller constituency than the President. To get reelected Congressman often must report to their communities that they did something to the people's benefit. Often members of Congress do so by including a pet project for his or her district, but if every member of Congress did this the budget would grow out of control very quickly, and often a Congressman cannot move to cut another Congressman's project without risking his or her own. The President by contrast has a national constituency thus does not risk reelection by offending a small number of Congressional districts or States. He can balance the budget by vetoing expenditures that are not truly of national importance as Andrew Jackson did when he vetoed the Maysville Road Bill.[88]

During the Clinton Administration the U.S. Congress passed the Line Item Veto Act of 1996 to give the President this power. However, the Supreme Court struck down this act in *Clinton v. City of New York*, holding that it violated the Presentment Clause which clearly delineated the process for passing a law.[89] Had Bill Clinton been President of the Confederacy the line item veto would have been within his executive discretion.

---

[88] Andrew Jackson's Veto of Maysville Road Bill (1830).

[89] 524 U.S. 417, 436-41 (1998).

(3)

> **Every order, resolution, or vote, to which the concurrence of both Houses may be necessary (except on a question of adjournment) shall be presented to the President of the Confederate States; and before the same shall take effect, shall be approved by him; or, being disapproved by him, shall be repassed by two-thirds of both Houses, according to the rules and limitations prescribed in case of a bill.**

> Every Order, Resolution, or Vote to which the Concurrence of the Senate and House of Representatives may be necessary (except on a question of Adjournment) shall be presented to the President of the United States; and before the Same shall take Effect, shall be approved by him, or being disapproved by him, shall be repassed by two thirds of the Senate and House of Representatives, according to the Rules and Limitations prescribed in the Case of a Bill.

Sec. 8.

The Congress shall have power-

(1)

> **To lay and collect taxes, duties, imposts, and excises for revenue, *necessary* to pay the debts, provide for the common defense, *and carry on the Government of the Confederate States; but no bounties shall be granted from the Treasury; nor shall any duties or taxes on importations from foreign nations be laid to promote or foster any branch of industry; and* all duties, imposts, and excises shall be uniform throughout the *Confederate* States.**

> The Congress shall have Power To lay and collect Taxes, Duties, Imposts and Excises, to pay the Debts and provide for the common Defence and general Welfare of

> the United States; but all Duties, Imposts and Excises
> shall be uniform throughout the United States;

The Union's Framers gave Congress taxing powers so it could independently raise revenue rather than rely on requisitions from the State governments.[90] The Confederate Framers answered a major concern Anti-Federalists had about this taxing and spending power. The Anti-Federalists believed that the term "general Welfare" was too subject to abuse as Congress could define whatever it pleased as "general Welfare" and then lay taxation for that purpose.[91]

During the drafting of the Constitution Union Framer Gouverneur Morris tried separating the taxing and spending clauses with a semicolon, making them to distinct powers.[92] However, another Framer Roger Sherman caught this and with the other delegates changed it to a comma.[93] In *United States v. Butler* the Supreme Court analyzed the differing opinions of James Madison and Alexander Hamilton on these clauses.[94] Madison asserted that "General Welfare" was a

---

[90] McDonald, *Novus Ordo Seclorum*, 170.

[91] "Centennial," Number I (October 5, 1787).

[92] McDonald, *Novus Ordo Seclorum*, 265.

[93] *Id.*

[94] 297 U.S. 1, 65 (1936).

reference to the other enumerated powers of Congress not relating to the "common Defence" thus Congress could only tax and spend for those purposes.[95] Hamilton argued that the two were separate powers and that Congress can tax and appropriate as it sees fit.[96] The Court adopted Hamilton's view[97] despite the aforementioned drafting history which favored Maddison's reading over Hamilton's.

Anti-Federalists feared that under the language of the Constitution Congress would be able to monopolize the taxing power by forbidding States to tax goods that Congress taxes or by raising Federal taxes would so high the that States would be unable to tax their citizens further.[98] Such a situation would make States totally dependent on Federal funding. Despite Maddison's answer that the Federal government would be more dependent on the States than vice-versa,[99] this fear to an extent has been proven true. In *South Dakota v. Dole* the Court approved of Congress placing conditions on States that receive Federal funding provided that

---

[95] *Id.*

[96] *Id.* at 65-66.

[97] *Id.* at 66.

[98] Pennsylvania Minority (December 18, 1787).

[99] THE FEDERALIST NO. 46 (James Maddison).

the condition is reasonably related to the purpose of the funding and the amount of the funds withheld is not coercive.[100]

The Confederates answered these concerns and adopted Maddison's reading of the Constitution by adding the word "necessary" and changing "general Welfare" to "carry on the Government of the Confederate States," expressly limiting the raising and spending of Confederate tax dollars to legitimate government functions.

The second change to this subsection is a restriction on the motivation behind certain taxes. Strict-constructionists of the Constitution argue that taxation can only be for the purpose of generating revenue for the government, not for the purpose of regulating conduct. Initially the U.S. Supreme Court partially endorsed this view in holding an excise tax on goods produced by child labor unconstitutional, noting that while there may be an incidental motive for raising a tax sometimes a tax's penalizing features reach the point that they become penalties rather than taxes.[101] However, in later cases the Court backed away from this stance, such as in *National Federation of Independent Business v. Sebelius* where the Individual Mandate of the Patient Protection and Affordable Care Act

---

[100] 483 U.S. 203, 207-11.

[101] *Child Labor Tax Case*, 259 U.S. 20, 38 (1922).

(aka Obamacare) requiring people to purchase health insurance or pay a tax was upheld.[102]

Before the Supreme Court addressed the issue, the motivation for levying tariffs almost led to a civil war in the Nullification Crisis of 1832-33. President John Quincy Adams signed the Tariff of 1828 (also known as the Tariff of Abominations) which was designed to protect American industry from foreign competition.[103] This was the first of three parts of Henry Clay's American System, the other two parts being Federally funded internal improvements and a national bank.[104] However, this tariff was damaging to the South's economy which was heavily dependent on trade with Europe.[105] Further, many considered the tariff to be unconstitutional because it was passed not for the purpose of generating revenue but to protect Northern industry from foreign competition.[106] A compromise tariff and Jackson's threatened use of force averted secession and civil war.[107] The

---

[102] 567 U.S. 519, 544-46 (2012).

[103] Richard E. Ellis, *The Union at Risk: Jacksonian Democracy, States' Rights, and the Nullification Crisis*, Oxford University Press: New York, NY 1987, 7, 42, 45.

[104] *Id.* at 19-20.

[105] *Id.* at 7.

[106] *Id.* at 43.

[107] *Id.* at 158-77.

Nullification Crisis was fresh in the minds of the Confederate Framers, so they included a clause expressly prohibiting protective tariffs, something that just recently became a controversy once again under President Donald Trump.

The Confederates also prohibited the payment of bounties. Georgia's Declaration of Causes Justifying Secession criticized bounties, declaring that they only benefited those in the North, not the South.[108]

(2)

> **To borrow money on the credit of the *Confederate* States.**

> To borrow Money on the credit of the United States;

(3)

> **To regulate commerce with foreign nations, and among the several States, and with the Indian tribes; *but neither this, nor any other clause contained in the Constitution, shall ever be construed to delegate the power to Congress to appropriate money for any internal improvement intended to facilitate commerce; except for the purpose of furnishing lights, beacons, and buoys, and other aids to navigation upon the coasts, and the improvement of harbors and the removing of obstructions in river navigation; in all which cases such duties shall be laid on the navigation facilitated thereby as may be necessary to pay the costs and expenses thereof.***

---

[108] Georgia's Declaration of Causes, https://web.archive.org/web/19980128034930/http://sunsite.utk.edu/civil-war/reasons.html (accessed April 3, 2018).

The Confederate Constitution

> To regulate Commerce with foreign Nations, and among
> the several States, and with the Indian Tribes;

The power to regulate commerce originated with the trade wars that many States engaged in under the Articles of Confederation as well as the desire to improve America's commercial standing in the world.[109]

The Confederate Framers rejected the second portion of Clay's American System by expressly prohibiting Federal expenditures financing internal improvements. Strict constructionists argued that funding for such projects was unconstitutional when not done in pursuance of Congress' enumerated powers.[110] Madison vetoed such a bill because he asked Congress to amend the Constitution first to authorize such expenditures, but Congress failed to do so.[111] Others thought it bad policy to take money from the general treasury and use it to finance a project that only benefits a State, or in some instances a single district within a State.[112] Georgia's Declaration of Causes made an explicit complaint about such expenditures benefitting the North at the South's expense given that most tariff

---

[109] Kathleen M. Sullivan and Gerald Gunther, *Constitutional Law*, 17th Ed., Foundation Press, New York, NY; 2010, 31; McDonald, *Novus Ordo Seclorum*, 169-70.

[110] Ellis, *Union at Risk*, 19-20; Andrew Jackson's Veto of Maysville Road Bill (1830).

[111] Gutzman, *The Politically Incorrect Guide to the Constitution*, 87-88.

[112] Andrew Jackson's Veto of Maysville Road Bill (1830).

revenue came from the South.[113] The Confederates made the implicit prohibition on Federally funded internal improvements explicit in their Constitution, but they also carved out limited exceptions that were of an interstate character but provided a limited source of funding for those projects: duties related to use of such improvements.

Other than this change the limits of Congress' Commerce Power were left unchanged from the Union version save any restriction elsewhere in the Confederate Constitution. Throughout U.S. history the Supreme Court's interpretation of the Commerce Clause varied between limiting and expanding Congress' commerce power. In *Gibbons v. Ogden* Chief Justice Marshall ruled that Congress could license people to use waterways and that States cannot interfere with that exercise.[114] Other sessions of the Court read the Commerce Clause much more narrowly, such as in *Hammer v. Dagenhart* where the Court ruled that Congress could not use its interstate commerce power to prevent the transportation of goods made by child labor across State lines as such a restriction

---

[113] Georgia's Declaration of Causes, https://web.archive.org/web/19980128034930/http://sunsite.utk.edu/civil-war/reasons.html (accessed April 3, 2018).

[114] 22 U.S. 1, 8 (1824).

was essentially a restriction on production rather than transportation.[115] During the New Deal this decision was reversed in *United States v. Darby*.[116]

The Court interpreted the commerce power even more broadly in *Wickard v. Filburn*[117] and again in *Gonzales v. Raich*[118] by allowing Congress to regulate intrastate commerce when it significantly affects interstate commerce, affirming Federal laws limiting wheat production and prohibiting marijuana production respectfully. However, the Court has limited the commerce power in other areas, such in *United States v. Lopez* where a law prohibiting carrying firearms within 1,000 feet of a school was found unconstitutional as it did not regulate economic activity and was too attenuated from interstate commerce.[119] The Court ruled in *Sebelius* that Congress cannot use its commerce power to compel people to participate in economic activity.[120]

---

[115] 247 U.S. 251, 271-72 (1918).

[116] 312 U.S. 100, 115-16 (1941).

[117] 317 U.S. 111, 117 (1942).

[118] 545 U.S. 1, 17 (2005).

[119] 514 U.S. 549, 561-68.

[120] 567 U.S. 519, 552.

The wording of the Confederate Commerce Clause allows for as broad or as narrow an interpretation as the U.S. Supreme Court has held during various points in American history and as litigants argue under the U.S. Commerce Clause today.

(4)

> **To establish uniform laws of naturalization, and uniform laws on the subject of bankruptcies, throughout the *Confederate* States; *but no law of Congress shall discharge any debt contracted before the passage of the same.***
>
> To establish an uniform Rule of Naturalization, and uniform Laws on the subject of Bankruptcies throughout the United States;

The Confederates placed a limitation on the discharge of debts in bankruptcy proceedings.

(5)

> **To coin money, regulate the value thereof, and of foreign coin, and fix the standard of weights and measures.**
>
> To coin Money, regulate the Value thereof, and of foreign Coin, and fix the Standard of Weights and Measures;

(6)

> **To provide for the punishment of counterfeiting the securities and current coin of the Confederate States.**
>
> To provide for the Punishment of counterfeiting the Securities and current Coin of the United States;

(7)

> **To establish post offices and post routes;** *but the
> expenses of the Post Office Department, after the 1st
> day of March in the year of our Lord eighteen hundred
> and sixty-three, shall be paid out of its own revenues.*

> To establish Post Offices and post Roads;

The Confederates decided that the postal service should be self-sufficient

thus the general government would only finance it for the first two years of its

existence. This answered another complaint raised in Georgia's Declaration of

Causes.[121]

(8)

> **To promote the progress of science and useful arts, by
> securing for limited times to authors and inventors
> the exclusive right to their respective writings and
> discoveries.**

> To promote the Progress of Science and useful Arts, by
> securing for limited Times to Authors and Inventors the
> exclusive Right to their respective Writings and
> Discoveries;

Maddison noted that this power was of unquestioned usefulness based on

English Common Law and that the States could not separately make effectual

---

[121] Georgia's Declaration of Causes,
https://web.archive.org/web/19980128034930/http://sunsite.utk.edu/civil-war/reasons.html (accessed April 3, 2018).

provisions.[122] The Supreme Court has yet to strike down a patent or copyright law for extending past "limited Times" despite growing criticism of companies, notably Disney, lobbying to have copyrights extended for greater periods of time.[123]

(9)

> **To constitute tribunals inferior to the Supreme Court.**
>
> To constitute Tribunals inferior to the supreme Court;

(10)

> **To define and punish piracies and felonies committed on the high seas, and offenses against the law of nations.**
>
> To define and punish Piracies and Felonies committed on the high Seas, and Offences against the Law of Nations;

(11)

> **To declare war, grant letters of marque and reprisal, and make rules concerning captures on land and water.**
>
> To declare War, grant Letters of Marque and Reprisal, and make Rules concerning Captures on Land and Water;

---

[122] THE FEDERALIST NO. 43.

[123] Robert P. Merges, Peter S. Menell, and Mark A. Lemley, *Intellectual Property in the New Technological Age*, Wolters Kluwer Law & Business: New York, NY 2012, 526-30.

The power to declare war traditionally belonged to the Crown under the British constitutional system. The Union Framers instead gave this power to Congress. Ever since Congress and the President struggled with each other as to how far the President's commander-in-chief power extends when Congress has not declared war.

(12)

> **To raise and support armies; but no appropriation of money to that use shall be for a longer term than two years.**
>
> To raise and support Armies, but no Appropriation of Money to that Use shall be for a longer Term than two Years;

A traditional Anglo-American belief was that a large standing army was the tool of a tyrant.[124] That is why the Founders of both Constitutions placed a restriction that an appropriation to fund the army can last for only two years, forcing Congress to reevaluate the cost and thus the size of the army with great frequency.[125] If the people feel that the government is misusing the army they can vote for Representatives that will not fund the army, resulting in the army being dismantled.

---

[124] Brutus X, January 24, 1788.

[125] McDonald, *Novus Ordo Seclorum*, 268.

Despite this protection the Anti-Federalists criticized the Constitution because it allowed a standing army to exist in a time of peace.[126] Hamilton defended the presence of standing army by arguing that otherwise the nation would be unable to defend itself in the event of attack and it would encourage compliance with national law.[127] He also stated that the government would have the power to create its own magistrates to enforce its laws and thus the army would not ordinarily be used to compel compliance as it would in a confederation.[128]

Hamilton predicted that under the Articles of Confederation if some States flouted national law the complying States might wage war against them, leading to the dissolution of the Union.[129] Ironically this prediction came to fruition under the Constitution: the South accused the North of non-compliance with the Constitution and seceded, resulting in the North accusing the South of non-compliance and crushing the South with a large army. Arguably the Union's conquest of the Confederacy proved the Anti-Federalists correct.

---

[126] Speech of James Wilson, October 6, 1787; Pennsylvania Minority, December 18, 1787.

[127] THE FEDERALIST NO. 16 (Alexander Hamilton).

[128] THE FEDERALIST NO. 27 (Alexander Hamilton).

[129] THE FEDERALIST NO. 16 (Alexander Hamilton).

The Civil War introduced the first national draft in both the Confederacy and the Union. Many people, including Confederate Vice President Alexander Stephens,[130] New York Governor Horatio Seymour, [131] and U.S. Chief Justice Roger Brooke Taney[132] decried the draft as unconstitutional. Abraham Lincoln defended the constitutionality of the draft by invoking this clause and noting that there was no limitation as to the means of raising armies, thus an army could be made of men serving voluntarily or involuntarily.[133] He further defended the draft as necessary to fight the war.[134] Jefferson Davis could have advanced the same arguments under his Constitution. During World War I the Supreme Court upheld the draft.[135]

(13)

To provide and maintain a navy.

---

[130] "Alexander H. Stephens," History, 2018 https://www.history.com/topics/american-civil-war/alexander-h-stephens (accessed April 12, 2018).

[131] Melvin I. Urofsky and Paul Finkelman, *Documents of American Constitutional & Legal History*, Oxford University Press: New York, NY 2008, 481.

[132] Gutzman, *The Politically Incorrect Guide to the Constitution*, 157.

[133] Abraham Lincoln, *Constitutionality of the Draft*, 1864.

[134] *Id.*

[135] *Aver v. United States*, 245 U.S. 366, 375-90 (1918).

To provide and maintain a Navy;

The English, living on an island, fostered a strong naval tradition, partly on the belief that a strong navy precluded the need for a strong army which as noted previously was often seen as the tool of a tyrant. Despite this many Anti-Federalists had a strong misgiving about a powerful navy, especially considering the Federal government's power over the army and purse.[136]

(14)

> **To make rules for the government and regulation of the land and naval forces.**
>
> To make Rules for the Government and Regulation of the land and naval Forces;

(15)

> **To provide for calling forth the militia to execute the laws of the *Confederate* States, suppress insurrections, and repel invasions.**
>
> To provide for calling forth the Militia to execute the Laws of the Union, suppress Insurrections and repel Invasions;

The Anti-Federalists criticized the ability of the Federal government to nationalize the militia as it could turn a State's own troops against it.[137] The Federalists defended this clause as necessary for national defense as in the event of

---

[136] Main, *The Anti-Federalists*, 16.
[137] The Speeches of Patrick Henry, June 5, 1788.

an invasion the militia of every State could be assembled to repel it, thus protecting the Union as a whole.[138] Some historians attribute the Confederacy's defeat to the failure of the States to send requested aid to the national government.

Abraham Lincoln invoked a statute passed pursuant to this clause when he called for 75,000 volunteers to suppress, "combinations too powerful to be suppressed by the ordinary course of judicial proceedings, or by the powers vested in the marshals by law."[139] This Proclamation and the Emancipation Proclamation referring to, "any State or designated part of a State, the people whereof shall then be in rebellion against the United States,"[140] calls to mind Hamilton's wording that a national army should be created in the event an, "insurrection should pervade a whole State, or principal part of it."[141] Another noteworthy nationalization of the State militia was when President Dwight D. Eisenhower nationalized the Arkansas National Guard during the Little Rock Integration dispute.

(16)

> **To provide for organizing, arming, and disciplining the militia, and for governing such part of them as**

---

[138] THE FEDERALIST NO. 4 (John Jay).

[139] "Proclamation for 75,000 Volunteers," April 15, 1861.

[140] "The Emancipation Proclamation," (January 1, 1863). http://www.historynet.com/emancipation-proclamation-text (accessed March 21, 2018).

[141] THE FEDERALIST NO. 28 (Alexander Hamilton).

may be employed in the service of the *Confederate* States; reserving to the States, respectively, the appointment of the officers, and the authority of training the militia according to the discipline prescribed by Congress.

To provide for organizing, arming, and disciplining, the Militia, and for governing such Part of them as may be employed in the Service of the United States, reserving to the States respectively, the Appointment of the Officers, and the Authority of training the Militia according to the discipline prescribed by Congress;

President James Knox Polk almost ran afoul of this clause when he offered to make Jefferson Davis a major general in the Mississippi militia during the Mexican-American War. Davis reminded Polk that only the State government could appoint militia officers, so instead he accepted Colonel's commission under Mississippi law. After he resigned from the Senate but before he became President of the Confederacy Davis was finally elected major general by the people of Mississippi.

(17)

> **To exercise exclusive legislation, in all cases whatsoever, over such district (not exceeding ten miles square) as may, by cession of one or more States and the acceptance of Congress, become the seat of the Government of the Confederate States; and to exercise like authority over all places purchased by the consent of the Legislature of the State in which the same shall be, for the erection of forts, magazines, arsenals, dockyards, and other needful buildings; and**

> To exercise exclusive Legislation in all Cases
> whatsoever, over such District (not exceeding ten Miles
> square) as may, by Cession of particular States, and the
> Acceptance of Congress, become the Seat of the
> Government of the United States, and to exercise like
> Authority over all Places purchased by the Consent of the
> Legislature of the State in which the Same shall be, for
> the Erection of Forts, Magazines, Arsenals, dock-Yards,
> and other needful Buildings;—And

Maddison stated that the ability of Congress to create a legislative district was necessary to avoid one State from having undue influence on the Federal government.[142] The United States government used the authority of this subsection to establish the District of Columbia as such a district with Washington City as the Union's capital. Previously Philadelphia, Pennsylvania and New York City served as the capitals of the United States. Despite having this power the Confederacy never created such a district, instead establishing first Montgomery, Alabama and then Richmond, Virginia as the capital city.

Disputed ownership of forts in the South was the issue that brought about the actual combat of the Civil War. When the Southern States seceded they declared that the United States government no longer had a right to keep such forts on their territory. Additionally, some argue that the United States breached its agreement

---

[142] THE FEDERALIST NO. 43 (James Maddison).

with South Carolina regarding Fort Sumter.[143] The agreement called for

construction of the fort to be completed within five years and the fort was to

properly garrisoned at all times.[144] Construction was still incomplete when the

Civil War started despite over five years having passed and the fort was not

garrisoned until South Carolina seceded.[145]

(18)

> **To make all laws which shall be necessary and proper
> for carrying into execution the foregoing powers, and
> all other powers vested by this Constitution in the
> Government of the Confederate States, or in any
> department or officer thereof.**

> To make all Laws which shall be necessary and proper
> for carrying into Execution the foregoing Powers, and all
> other Powers vested by this Constitution in the
> Government of the United States, or in any Department
> or Officer thereof.

Despite their States' Rights stance the Confederate Framers left in the

controversial Necessary and Proper Clause that was so despised by the Anti-

Federalists[146] and utilized by Alexander Hamilton[147] and John Marshall to argue

---

[143] John C. Whatley, "South Carolina Takes Back Her Fort," *Alabama Confederate*, Vol. 30, No. 3, July 2011.

[144] *Id.*

[145] *Id.*

[146] Brutus I, VI, and X, October 18, 1787, December 27, 1787, and January 31, 1788.

for implied powers of the Federal government in cases such as the *M'Culloch* decision.[148] The Anti-Federalists feared that the Courts would use this clause to give too much deference to Congress in its use of powers by defining whatever it wished as "necessary and proper."[149] Perhaps the *M'Culloch* decision proved them right.

Hamilton defended this clause as necessary to ensure that Congress could carry out its other enumerated powers, declaring that it gives Congress the power to choose the means to execute its powers.[150] Hamilton answered the Anti-Federalist criticism by arguing that while the national government is the first judge of what is necessary and proper the people have the means to stop Congress should it overstep its bounds.[151] Maddison added that the Constitution could not practically specify the various means for Congress to carry out its powers thus such a clause was necessary.[152]

---

[147] Alexander Hamilton, *Opinion as to the Constitutionality of the Bank of the United States*, 1791.

[148] 17 U.S. 316, 324.

[149] Brutus XI, January 31, 1788.

[150] THE FEDERALIST NO. 33-34 (Alexander Hamilton).

[151] THE FEDERALIST NO. 33 (Alexander Hamilton).

[152] THE FEDERALIST NO. 44 (James Maddison).

Sec. 9.

(1)

> *The importation of negroes of the African race from any foreign country other than the slaveholding States or Territories of the United States of America, is hereby forbidden; and Congress is required to pass such laws as shall effectually prevent the same.*

(2)

> **Congress shall also have power to prohibit the introduction of slaves from any State not a member of, or Territory not belonging to, this Confederacy.**

> The Migration or Importation of such Persons as any of the States now existing shall think proper to admit, shall not be prohibited by the Congress prior to the Year one thousand eight hundred and eight, but a Tax or duty may be imposed on such Importation, not exceeding ten dollars for each Person.

The Union Constitution gave Congress the discretion to continue allowing slaves to be imported into the United States or to prohibit it starting in 1808 and to tax slaves until 1808to discourage people from purchasing them.[153] This clause was proposed by Luther Martin who thought it necessary as slaves were counted towards representation thus encouraging the purchase of slaves, weakening one part of the Union that the other parts were bound to protect. [154] He also thought

---

[153] THE FEDERALIST NO. 42 (James Maddison).

[154] Slavery and the Constitution, August 21-22, 1787.

that slavery was inconsistent with the values of the American Revolution.[155] Roger Sherman concurred in this as a compromise offer to John Rutledge, keeping the slave trade open for another twenty years and providing for the recovery of fugitive slaves in exchange for a tariff compromise.[156]

Some Southern States wanted the slave trade kept open so that they could import more slaves, and some Northern States also wanted it open to benefit their shipping industry.[157] Other States North and South wanted to abolish it for a variety of reasons such as preserving a local monopoly, easing the gradual abolition of slavery, and preventing slave rebellions.[158] Congress and President Thomas Jefferson closed the international slave trade in 1808.[159] By then most Americans had come to accept slavery as a fact of life for those born into it, but not

---

[155] *Id.*

[156] Gutzman, *The Politically Incorrect Guide to the Constitution*, 114.

[157] Slavery and the Constitution, August 21-22, 1787.

[158] *Id.*

[159] Dumas Malone, *Jefferson and His Time Volume Five: Jefferson the President Second Term 1805-1809*, Little, Brown, & Co.: Boston, MA 1974, 541.

the future enslavement of additional people.[160] Many Union Framers believed that

slavery would one day die out in the United States.[161]

The Confederate Constitution codified this prohibition, requiring Congress

to prohibit the importation of slaves from any nation other than the United States.

Apparently the Confederates wanted good relations with the slave States that

remained in the Union. However, Congress could still prohibit the importation of

slaves from certain U.S. States of territories. Some Confederate Framers wanted to

reopen the slave trade, but they were overruled, possibly for the same reasons some

Southerners wanted to close the slave trade in 1787.

(3)

> **The privilege of the writ of habeas corpus shall not be suspended, unless when in cases of rebellion or invasion the public safety may require it.**

> The Privilege of the Writ of Habeas Corpus shall not be suspended, unless when in Cases of Rebellion or Invasion the public Safety may require it.

Both Constitutions allow Congress to suspend the writ of habeas corpus in

the event of invasion or rebellion. Throughout English history both Kings and the

Protectorate (the government of England during the interregnum following the

---

[160] McDonald, *Novus Ordo Seclorum*, 52.

[161] Slavery and the Constitution, August 21-22, 1787.

English Civil War) engaged in arbitrary arrests, leading the passage of Habeas Corpus Act of 1679 to prevent such arrests.[162]

The Anti-Federalists criticized this clause as the Federal government may use a crisis in one State, such as Georgia, to justify suspending habeas corpus in a distant State, such as Massachusetts.[163] As it turns out they were right. Both Abraham Lincoln and Jefferson Davis suspended habeas corpus in their respective countries during the Civil War, and both were condemned for it. It should be noted that Davis got permission from his Congress before doing so,[164] but Lincoln got it after.[165]

Before Congress authorized Lincoln to do so, Chief Justice Roger Brooke Taney in his capacity as a circuit judge ruled in *Ex parte Merryman* that only Congress, not the President, has the power to suspend habeas corpus.[166] Chief Justice Taney noted that this clause is in Article I dealing with Congress, not

---

[162] McDonald, *Novus Ordo Seclorum*, 37-38.

[163] "John DeWitt," October 27, 1787.

[164] Donald R. McClarey, "Jefferson Davis and the Suspension of Habeas Corpus," The American Catholic, February 7, 2017 http://the-american-catholic.com/2013/02/07/jefferson-davis-and-the-suspension-of-habeas-corpus/ (accessed March 21, 2018).

[165] Habeas Corpus Suspension Act, 12 Stat. 755 (1863)

[166] 17 F.Cas. 144, 148 (Circuit Court, MD 1861).

Article II dealing with the President.[167] Taney further declared that suspension of habeas corpus does not override other constitutional rights such as entitlement to due process.[168] In *Ex parte Milligan* the Supreme Court invalidated the suspension of habeas corpus in Indiana, a State that was not part of the Confederacy or invaded by the Confederacy.[169] The Court held that that martial law cannot be enacted from a threatened invasion, only an actual, present invasion.[170] However, during World War II the Court backed away from this stance when it upheld the validity of the internment of Japanese-Americans in *Korematsu v. United States*.[171] In *Trump v. Hawaii* the Supreme Court declared that its decision in *Korematsu* was wrong.[172]

(4)

> **No bill of attainder, ex post facto law,** *or law denying or impairing the right of property in negro slaves shall be passed.*

> No Bill of Attainder or ex post facto Law shall be passed.

---

[167] *Id.*

[168] *Id.* at 149.

[169] 71 U.S. 2, 80 (1866).

[170] *Id.*

[171] 323 U.S. 214, 217-20 (1944).

[172] 584 U.S. ___ (2018)

The first two protections in the clause stem from past English abuses. Before the Glorious Revolution of 1688 the English Parliament would sometimes pass Acts of Attainder, laws declaring a person guilty of a crime, usually treason, and determining a punishment. After the Glorious Revolution these laws were prohibited as they gave the accused no opportunity to defend himself.

The prohibition on ex post facto laws likely derived from how early in Parliament's history criminal laws were made retroactive to the start of the session of Parliament. This was fundamentally unfair as it expected people to anticipate what laws Parliament will pass once the next session started. A person may do something that was perfectly legal at the time he did it, but then Parliament retroactively declared it illegal. The prohibition on ex post facto laws only applies to criminal laws, not civil offenses.[173]

Unsurprisingly, as most of the debates leading up to the South's secession centered around slavery the Confederate Framers put in a clause prohibiting the Federal Congress of the CSA from passing laws that could impair slavery rights.[174] Many U.S. Founding Fathers struggled with the issue over slavery. Washington,

---

[173] McDonald, *Novus Ordo Seclorum*, 272.

[174] Declaration of Causes of Seceding States, https://web.archive.org/web/19980128034930/http://sunsite.utk.edu/civil-war/reasons.html (accessed April 3, 2018); Florida Draft Declaration of Causes, http://www.civilwarcauses.org/florida-dec.htm (accessed April 3, 2018).

Maddison, and Jefferson detested it as incompatible with American liberty and equality, but they saw no practical way to destroy it in their time.[175] Others like Charles Pickney looked to historic examples of slave-based republics such as Greece and Rome as justification for continued slavery.[176] Confederate Vice President Alexander Stephens infamously declared slavery to be the "cornerstone" on which the Confederacy was built,[177] but after the Civil War he was forced to partially retract this statement.[178]

It was already implicit in the U.S. Constitution prior to the Thirteenth Amendment that slavery was a States' Rights issue.[179] Abraham Lincoln himself denied having the authority to interfere with slavery rights and endorsed a proposed constitutional amendment that would have forever protected slavery in

---

[175] McDonald, *Novus Ordo Seclorum*, 50.

[176] Slavery and the Constitution, August 21-22, 1787.

[177] Alexander Stephens, *Cornerstone Speech*, (March 21, 1861), https://web.archive.org/web/20130822142313/http://teachingamericanhistory.org/library/document/cornerstone-speech/ (accessed June 18, 2017).

[178] Alexander Stephens, Cornerstone Retraction, http://cwmemory.com/2013/01/23/alexander-stephens-reinforces-the-cornerstone/ (accessed June 19, 2017).

[179] Slavery and the Constitution, August 21-22, 1787.

States that chose to allow it.[180] The Corwin Amendment, named for its author

Representative Thomas Corwin of Ohio, stated:

> No amendment shall be made to the Constitution which
> will authorize or give to Congress the power to abolish or
> interfere, within any State, with the domestic institutions
> thereof, including that of persons held to labor or service
> by the laws of said State.[181]

Instead of accepting this compromise the South seceded, the Civil War began, and

within two years Lincoln went back on his previous promise to protect slavery and

instead issued his likely unconstitutional Emancipation Proclamation declaring

slaves under Confederate control to be free.[182] Knowing that constitutional

challenges to his proclamation were looming as well as the fact that it left slaves in

Union territory untouched Lincoln promoted the Thirteenth Amendment which

Congress proposed and the States ratified:

> Section 1: Neither slavery nor involuntary servitude,
> except as a punishment for crime whereof the party shall
> have been duly convicted, shall exist within the United
> States, or any place subject to their jurisdiction.

---

[180] Abraham Lincoln, First Inaugural Address, (March 4, 1861). http://avalon.law.yale.edu/19th_century/ lincoln1.asp (accessed March 2, 2013).

[181] "Constitutional Amendments Not Ratified," United States House of Representatives, https://web.archive.org/web/20120702135703/http://www.house.gov/house/Amendnotrat.shtml (accessed March 21, 2018).

[182] "The Emancipation Proclamation," (January 1, 1863).

(5)

> **No capitation or other direct tax shall be laid, unless in proportion to the census or enumeration hereinbefore directed to be taken.**
>
> No Capitation, or other direct, Tax shall be laid, unless in Proportion to the Census or Enumeration herein before directed to be taken.

The Union version was altered by the Sixteenth Amendment.

(6)

> **No tax or duty shall be laid on articles exported from any State, *except by a vote of two-thirds of both Houses.***
>
> No Tax or Duty shall be laid on Articles exported from any State.

The Confederate Congress gained the ability to tax goods imported from the States provided two-thirds of both Houses of Congress agreed. This went against the intent of the Union Framers who feared that their own States' goods might be taxed.[183]

(7)

> **No preference shall be given by any regulation of commerce or revenue to the ports of one State over those of another.**
>
> No Preference shall be given by any Regulation of Commerce or Revenue to the Ports of one State over

---

[183] McDonald, *Novus Ordo Seclorum*, 263.

those of another: nor shall Vessels bound to, or from, one State, be obliged to enter, clear, or pay Duties in another.

The Union Framers placed some restrictions on Congress' commerce power, such as preventing Congress from favoring one State's ports over another's.[184] The Confederates eliminated the clause prohibiting States from charging duties on ships from fellow member States of the Confederacy.

(8)

> **No money shall be drawn from the Treasury, but in consequence of appropriations made by law; and a regular statement and account of the receipts and expenditures of all public money shall be published from time to time.**

> No Money shall be drawn from the Treasury, but in Consequence of Appropriations made by Law; and a regular Statement and Account of the Receipts and Expenditures of all public Money shall be published from time to time.

(9)

> **Congress shall appropriate no money from the Treasury except by a vote of two-thirds of both Houses, taken by yeas and nays, unless it be asked and estimated for by some one of the heads of departments and submitted to Congress by the President; or for the purpose of paying its own expenses and contingencies; or for the payment of claims against the Confederate States, the justice of which shall have been judicially declared by a tribunal for the investigation of claims against the**

---

[184] *Id.*

Government, which it is hereby made the duty of Congress to establish.

This clause was added to limit the Confederate Congress' ability to appropriate money. As noted before, an Anti-Federalist concern was that if the Federal government was allowed to create debt at its discretion it could use that debt to justify more taxes.

(10)

> **All bills appropriating money shall specify in Federal currency the exact amount of each appropriation and the purposes for which it is made; and Congress shall grant no extra compensation to any public contractor, officer, agent, or servant, after such contract shall have been made or such service rendered.**

As with the previous clause, this was added to promote fiscal responsibility by the Confederate Congress.

(11)

> **No title of nobility shall be granted by the Confederate States; and no person holding any office of profit or trust under them shall, without the consent of the Congress, accept of any present, emolument, office, or title of any kind whatever, from any king, prince, or foreign state.**

> No Title of Nobility shall be granted by the United States: And no Person holding any Office of Profit or Trust under them, shall, without the Consent of the Congress, accept of any present, Emolument, Office, or Title, of any kind whatever, from any King, Prince, or foreign State.

These provisions confirmed America's republican nature.[185] One proposed amendment to the United States Constitution would have required U.S. citizens to reject titles of titles of nobility from foreign governments unless they received permission from Congress. They would lose their U.S. citizenship if they accepted such titles without the consent of Congress. This amendment was never ratified by the States, but it read:

> If any citizen of the United States shall accept, claim, receive or retain any title of nobility or honour, or shall, without the consent of Congress, accept and retain any present, pension, office or emolument of any kind whatever, from any emperor, king, prince or foreign power, such person shall cease to be a citizen of the United States, and shall be incapable of holding any office of trust or profit under them, or either of them.[186]

(12)

> **Congress shall make no law respecting an establishment of religion, or prohibiting the free exercise thereof; or abridging the freedom of speech, or of the press; or the right of the people peaceably to assemble and petition the Government for a redress of grievances.**

---

[185] McDonald, *Novus Ordo Seclorum*, 268.

[186] "Constitutional Amendments Not Ratified," United States House of Representatives, https://web.archive.org/web/20120702135703/http://www.house.gov/house/Amendnotrat.shtml (accessed March 21, 2018).

The Confederate Constitution

The Confederates, as the authors of a new Constitution, incorporated the first twelve amendments to the United States Constitution directly into the new Constitution. This answered the Anti-Federalist criticism that the original U.S. Constitution did not have a Bill of Rights and that amending the Constitution to add one might not happen.[187] The preceding section correlates to the Union's First Amendment.

> Congress shall make no law respecting an establishment of religion, or prohibiting the free exercise thereof; or abridging the freedom of speech, or of the press; or the right of the people peaceably to assemble, and to petition the Government for a redress of grievances.

Being located in Article I, Section 9 the Confederate Bill of Rights expressly only limited the Federal Congress of the Confederacy, not the individual States. In the United States Chief Justice John Marshall ruled in *Barron v. City of Baltimore* that the Fifth Amendment to the United States Constitution, and by extension all of the Bill of Rights, only applied to the Federal government, not the States.[188] However, since the adoption of the Fourteenth Amendment to the United States Constitution the Supreme Court has gradually applied most of the Bill of Rights to

---

[187] "John DeWitt," October 27, 1787; Patrick Henry, June 5, 1788; Pennsylvania Minority, December 18, 1787.

[188] 32 U.S. 243, 250-51 (1833).

the States via the Fourteenth Amendment's Due Process Clause.[189] Because the

Fourteenth Amendment is not part of the Confederate Constitution, the doctrine of

incorporation would not apply in the Confederacy.

The religion clauses were adopted in response to the brutal history of

religious intolerance that plagued England and the rest of Europe.[190] The

Establishment Clause was also designed to protect State-sponsored Churches from

the creation of a national church which under the Supremacy Clause might

undermine State churches.[191]

The U.S. Supreme Court has interpreted the First Amendment extensively.

It is not unreasonable to assume that had the Confederacy survived its counterpart

would be interpreted in similar ways, albeit only applicable to the Federal

government. Many cases such as the school prayer and public display cases would

not come about in the Confederacy. The U.S. Supreme Court has rejected prayer

in public schools in cases such as *Engel v. Vitale*.[192] The Court is inconsistent

regarding public displays such as the Ten Commandments, approving them in

---

[189] E.g. *Gitlow v. People of the State of New York*, 268 U.S. 652, 664 (1925).

[190] McDonald, *Novus Ordo Seclorum*, 41-42.

[191] Gutzman, *The Politically Incorrect Guide to the Constitution*, 176-77, 183.

[192] 370 U.S. 421, 424-25 (1962).

cases such as *Van Orden v. Perry*[193] but disapproving them in others such as in *McCreary County, Ky. v. American Civil Liberties Union of Ky.*,[194] depending on the context. Also, as noted previously the Confederate Preamble would preclude any challenge to a reference to God in a Federal forum.

Like with the Establishment Clause the Free Exercise Clause would be seldom litigated in the Confederate Courts because the States interact with the people the most, thus the States of the Confederacy would only be limited by their State Constitutions. However, if there was ever Federal interplay with religion perhaps the Confederate Supreme Court would have interpreted this clause the same way as the Union Supreme Court. For example, in *Reynolds v. United States* the Supreme Court upheld a Federal law that prohibited polygamous marriage in the territory of the United States, holding that while freedom of religion protects beliefs it does not always protect practices.[195] "Congress was deprived of all legislative power over mere opinion, but was left free to reach actions which were in violation of social duties or subversive of good order."[196] However, sometimes the Court still ruled in favor of freedom of religion, such as in *Wisconsin v. Yoder*

---

[193] 545 U.S. 677, 691 (2005).

[194] 545 U.S. 844, 861 (2005).

[195] 98 U.S. 145, 162-63 (1876).

[196] *Id.* at 164.

where the Court ruled that the State could not force Amish parents to send their children to high school.[197] The Court modified *Yoder* in *Employment Division, Department of Human Resources v. Smith* by ruling that freedom of religion does not excuse one from compliance with an otherwise valid law, upholding the denial of unemployment benefits to a man who smoke peyote in a religious ceremony.[198] Recently in *Masterpiece Cakeshop, Ltd., et al. v. Colorado Civil Rights Commission et al.* the Supreme Court ruled that when the government weighs society's interest against a religious freedom claim it must do so in a neutral manner that is not hostile to a religious belief.[199]

Freedom of speech and petition originated as rights of members of the English House of Commons to speak in Parliament without fear of reprisal.[200] Over time this right developed into a personal right confirmed by the English Bill of Rights of 1689.[201] The Articles of Confederation guaranteed to the right of members of Congress to speak and debate in Congress.[202]

----

[197] 406 U.S. 205, 234-36 (1972).

[198] 494 U.S. 872, 878-79 (1990).

[199] 584 U.S. ___ (2018).

[200] McDonald, *Novus Ordo Seclorum*, 39.

[201] *Id.*

[202] Articles of Confederation of 1781, art. V.

The Supreme Court ruled in *Schenk v. United States* that freedom of speech is not absolute; for example it does not protect a man from falsely shouting fire in a crowded theater.[203] The Court adopted a clear and present danger test to determine when Congress can and cannot regulate speech.[204] Later in *Brandenburg v. Ohio* the Court narrowed this ruling to distinguish between mere advocacy of unlawful activity and incitement to imminent lawless action.[205] The Supreme Court applies strict scrutiny (requiring the least restrictive means) to restrictions on some forms of speech such as political speech.[206] Other forms of speech such as advertisements receive less protection and do not require the least restrictive means.[207] Some forms of speech such as obscenity have no protection under freedom of speech.[208]

The tradition of freedom of the press originally only referred to a freedom from prior restraint, not freedom from consequences of the thing published, such as

---

[203] 249 U.S. 47, 52 (1919).

[204] *Id.*

[205] 395 U.S. 444, 448-49 (1969).

[206] *Burson v. Freeman*, 504 U.S. 191, 198 (1992).

[207] E.g. commercial advertising. See *City of Cincinnati v. Discovery Network*, 507 U.S. 410, 417 (1993).

[208] *Miller v. California*, 413 U.S. 15, 23 (1973).

libel and sedition.[209] However, the Supreme Court ruled in *New York Times Co. v. Sullivan* that when public officers are criticized by the press the official cannot sue for libel without first showing that a false statement was made with actual malice or a reckless disregard for the truth.[210] The Supreme Court ruled in *Branzburg v. Hayes* that news reporters cannot hide behind the freedom of speech and press to refuse to identify their sources when required by law.[211]

(13)

> **A well-regulated militia being necessary to the security of a free State, the right of the people to keep and bear arms shall not be infringed.**

The Second Amendment to the U.S. Constitution:

> A well regulated Militia, being necessary to the security of a free State, the right of the people to keep and bear Arms, shall not be infringed.

Because many Americans of the Founding generation feared a large standing army they saw a militia made of ordinary citizens as the best way to protect the people.[212] The Supreme Court of the United States declared in *District of Columbia v. Heller* that this provision conferred an individual though not unlimited

---

[209] McDonald, *Novus Ordo Seclorum*, 48.

[210] 376 U.S. 254, 279-80 (1964).

[211] 408 U.S. 665, 682 (1972).

[212] McDonald, *Novus Ordo Seclorum*, 267.

right to keep and bear arms, invalidating a District of Columbia law prohibiting the possession of handguns in private homes.[213] The Court later extended this protection to the States in *MacDonald v. City of Chicago, Ill.*[214] However, as noted before the Fourteenth Amendment was not part of the Confederate Constitution, so only the Confederate Congress would be constrained by this clause.

(14)

> **No soldier shall, in time of peace, be quartered in any house without the consent of the owner; nor in time of war, but in a manner to be prescribed by law.**

The Union's Third Amendment:

> No Soldier shall, in time of peace be quartered in any house, without the consent of the Owner, nor in time of war, but in a manner to be prescribed by law.

This was a reaction to the Colonial era where British troops were quartered in private homes during times of peace.[215]

(15)

> **The right of the people to be secure in their persons, houses, papers, and effects, against unreasonable searches and seizures, shall not be violated; and no warrants shall issue but upon probable cause, supported by oath or affirmation, and particularly**

---

[213] 554 U.S. 570, 595 (2008).

[214] 561 U.S. 742, 791 (2010).

[215] THE DECLARATION OF INDEPENDENCE para. 16 (U.S. 1776).

describing the place to be searched and the persons or things to be seized.

The Union's Fourth Amendment:

> The right of the people to be secure in their persons, houses, papers, and effects, against unreasonable searches and seizures, shall not be violated, and no Warrants shall issue, but upon probable cause, supported by Oath or affirmation, and particularly describing the place to be searched, and the persons or things to be seized.

This amendment had its origin in the Writs of Assistance, open-ended search warrants that allowed British agents to search Colonial vessels to crack down on smuggling in the days leading up to the Revolution.[216] Attorney James Otis condemned these Writs of Assistance as violations of traditional English liberty.[217] The Union's Founders had these writs in mind when they wrote the Fourth Amendment.

In *Katz v. United States* the Supreme Court ruled that the Fourth Amendment protects people, not places, and only protects what they seek to keep private, not what they expose to the public.[218] Searches conducted without judicial

---

[216] Urofsky and Finkelman, *Documents of American Constitutional & Legal History*, 38.

[217] James Otis, *Against the Writs of Assistance*, 1761.

[218] 389 U.S. 347, 351 (1967).

approval via a warrant are per se unreasonable.[219] However, because the ultimate touchstone of the Fourth Amendment is reasonableness there are many exceptions to this rule, such as searches incident to arrests made in public,[220] stop and frisk upon reasonable suspicion one is engaged in a crime and is armed and dangerous,[221] and exigent circumstances.[222]

To enforce the Fourth Amendment the Supreme Court adopted a rule in *Weeks v. United States* that excluded illegally seized evidence from trial.[223] The Court subsequently applied the exclusionary rule to the States in *Mapp v. Ohio*.[224] While the Confederate Supreme Court might have reached similar interpretations of its own protection against unreasonable searches and seizures, such limitations would only constrain the Federal government.

However, the exclusionary rule is subject to much criticism. As Justice Clarence Thomas recently argued in his concurrence in *Collins v. Virginia* the

---

[219] *Id.* at 357.

[220] *United States v. Watson*, 423 U.S. 411, 423-24 (1976); *Chimel v. California*, 395 U.S. 752, 763 (1969).

[221] *Terry v. Ohio*, 392 U.S. 1, 27 (1968).

[222] *Brigham City, Utah v. Stuart*, 547 U.S. 398, 403 (2006).

[223] 232 U.S. 383, 393 (1914).

[224] 367 U.S. 643, 654 (1961).

exclusionary rule has no origin in the text of the Constitution or the history surrounding Fourth Amendment issues.[225] For the first century of the Fourth Amendment's existence the only remedy for a Fourth Amendment violation was a lawsuit in civil court.[226] Perhaps a Confederate Supreme Court staffed by Justices like Thomas, who is incidentally from the former Confederate State of Georgia, would have not adopted the exclusionary rule.

(16)

> **No person shall be held to answer for a capital or otherwise infamous crime, unless on a presentment or indictment of a grand jury, except in cases arising in the land or naval forces, or in the militia, when in actual service in time of war or public danger; nor shall any person be subject for the same offense to be twice put in jeopardy of life or limb; nor be compelled, in any criminal case, to be a witness against himself; nor be deprived of life, liberty, or property without due process of law; nor shall private property be taken for public use, without just compensation.**

The U.S. Fifth Amendment:

> No person shall be held to answer for a capital, or otherwise infamous crime, unless on a presentment or indictment of a Grand Jury, except in cases arising in the land or naval forces, or in the Militia, when in actual service in time of War or public danger; nor shall any person be subject for the same offence to be twice put in jeopardy of life or limb; nor shall be compelled in any

---

[225] 584 U.S. ___ (2018)(Thomas, J., concurring).

[226] *Id.*

criminal case to be a witness against himself, nor be
deprived of life, liberty, or property, without due process
of law; nor shall private property be taken for public use,
without just compensation.

Protection against double jeopardy is a right that developed in English law.[227] The Double Jeopardy Clause protects one from a second prosecution after an acquittal, a second prosecution after conviction (excepting retrial following a vacated conviction), and it protects against multiple punishments for the same offense.[228] Whether an act constitutes one offense or two is determined by whether each offense requires separate proof of a different element; if one offense has all the elements of another, then it is only one crime.[229]

The right against self-incrimination not only includes the right to not take the stand at trial but also the right to not make statements to the police during interrogation.[230] Police must take care to inform suspects held in custody of their right to not make a statement.[231]

---

[227] McDonald, *Novus Ordo Seclorum*, 39.

[228] *North Carolina v. Pearce*, 395 U.S. 711, 717 (1969).

[229] *United States v. Blockburger*, 284 U.S. 299, 304 (1932).

[230] *Miranda v. Arizona*, 384 U.S. 436, 444 (1966).

[231] *Id.*

The Supreme Court has given two interpretations of the Due Process Clause. The first is procedural due process, the requirement that before life, liberty, or property be taken away an individual must be afforded an opportunity to be heard.[232] An example of this is when laws are voided for vagueness: one must be on notice of what is illegal before one can be prosecuted.[233] The other is substantive due process first elaborated on in the infamous *Dred Scott v. Sandford* case, finding it unconstitutional to exclude property rights in slaves in the territories of the United States.[234] Substantive due process from the Fourteenth Amendment's Due Process Clause was later used to establish implied constitutional rights such as in *Griswold v. Connecticut* which established the right to privacy[235] and apply the Bill of Rights to the States. The Court has also used the Due Process Clause to require special actions by prosecutors in criminal cases, such as requiring the disclosure of exculpatory evidence to the defendant.[236] Many

---

[232] E.g. *Goldberg v. Kelly*, 397 U.S. 254, 262-63 (1970).

[233] *Papachristou v. City of Jacksonville*, 405 U.S. 156, 162 (1972).

[234] 60 U.S. 393, 450 (1857).

[235] 381 U.S. 479, 485 (1965).

[236] *Brady v. Maryland*, 373 U.S. 83, 86 (1963).

scholars and jurists criticize the substantive due process doctrine as a flawed doctrine not justified by the text of the Due Process Clauses.[237]

The government's traditional power of eminent domain to take private property for public use[238] was confirmed by the Fifth Amendment, but the U.S. Founding Fathers added, and the Confederates retained, a requirement that just compensation be paid. However, the government gets much leeway in defining what constitutes public use.[239]

As with the rest of the Confederate Bill of Rights, these protections only extend to Federal action.

(17)

> **In all criminal prosecutions the accused shall enjoy the right to a speedy and public trial, by an impartial jury of the State and district wherein the crime shall have been committed, which district shall have been previously ascertained by law, and to be informed of the nature and cause of the accusation; to be confronted with the witnesses against him; to have compulsory process for obtaining witnesses in his favor; and to have the assistance of counsel for his defense.**

The Union's Sixth Amendment:

---

[237] Antonin Scalia, *A Matter of Interpretation*, Princeton University Press: 1997, 24.

[238] McDonald, *Novus Ordo Seclorum*, 22.

[239] *Kelo v. City of New London*, 545 U.S. 469, 476-80 (2005).

> In all criminal prosecutions, the accused shall enjoy the right to a speedy and public trial, by an impartial jury of the State and district wherein the crime shall have been committed, which district shall have been previously ascertained by law, and to be informed of the nature and cause of the accusation; to be confronted with the witnesses against him; to have compulsory process for obtaining witnesses in his favor, and to have the Assistance of Counsel for his defence.

This amendment was likely a response to English laws dating prior to the reign of Mary I (1553-1558) prohibiting the retention of counsel, the right to testify, and the right to confront witnesses in capital cases.[240] Initially defense witnesses were not put under oath, giving them less credence than the Crown Prosecutor's witnesses, but by the reign of Queen Anne (1702-1714) defendants in treason and felony trials were given the right to have their witnesses testify under oath.[241]

The Supreme Court struggled with defining what constitutes a speedy trial violation, noting in *Barker v. Wingo* that the right is "necessarily relative...consistent with delays and depends on circumstances."[242] The Court adopted a balancing test requiring evaluations of claimed speedy trial violations to

---

[240] McDonald, *Novus Ordo Seclorum*, 38.

[241] *Id.*

[242] 407 U.S. 514, 521-22 (1972).

look at the length of the delay, the reason for the delay, the defendant's assertion of the right, and if the defendant was prejudiced by the delay.[243]

The Supreme Court observed in *Waller v. Georgia* that public trials encourage responsibility by government actors, encourage witnesses to come forward, and they discourage perjury.[244] However, the trial may be closed to the public if there is an overriding interest that is likely to be prejudiced by a public trial, the closure is no broader than necessary to protect that interest, the trial court considered reasonable alternatives to closure, and it made findings adequate to support the closure.[245]

In all cases where a defendant is exposed to more than six months of incarceration he or she is entitled to a jury trial.[246] Juries decide questions of fact in trials. This includes whether the defendant committed every element of the offense charged and any fact that could enhance a defendant's sentence, other than prior convictions, the jury must make that finding.[247] Even though the common law rule was for a jury to have twelve jurors, it can have as few as six people but

---

[243] *Id.* at 530.

[244] 467 U.S. 39, 46 (1984).

[245] *Id.* at 48.

[246] *Dyke v. Taylor Implement MFG. Co., Inc.*, 391 U.S. 216, 220 (1968).

[247] *Apprendi v. New Jersey*, 530 U.S. 466, 476-79 (2000).

no fewer.[248] The U.S. Supreme Court applied this right to the States,[249] but as noted previously the Confederate Bill of Rights did not apply to the States.

The right to confront witnesses includes the right to cross-examine a codefendant who confessed to the crime and implicated the defendant.[250] It also precludes the government from using testimonial hearsay (out of court statements offered to prove the truth of the matter asserted) in a criminal trial unless the declarant is unavailable and the defendant had a prior opportunity to cross-examine the declarant.[251]

Supreme Court jurisprudence on the right to counsel evolved over time. Initially people understood the right to only be the right to hire an attorney, not get one at the public expense. This changed in *Johnson v. Zerbst* when the Court ruled that a person could not be convicted in Federal court unless represented by counsel or the accused waived counsel.[252] In *Powell v. Alabama* when the Court indicated

---

[248] *Williams v. Florida*, 399 U.S. 78, 86 (1970); *Ballew v. Georgia*, 435 U.S. 223, 239 (1978).

[249] *Duncan v. Louisiana*, 391 U.S. 145, 148-49 (1968).

[250] *Bruton v. United States*, 391 U.S. 123, 126 (1968).

[251] *Crawford v. Washington*, 541 U.S. 36, 51-52 (2004).

[252] 304 U.S. 458, 462-63 (1938).

that in some instances due process required State courts to appoint counsel.[253]

However, the Court ruled in *Betts v. Brady* that the Sixth Amendment did not

require appointment of counsel in every case, instead looking to the individual

circumstances of the case to determine if due process required appointment of

counsel.[254] The Court reversed *Betts* in *Gideon v. Wainwright* and ruled that all of

anyone facing incarceration is entitled to appointment of counsel if indigent.[255]

The Court further ruled in *Strickland v. Washington* that the right to counsel

includes the right to competent counsel.[256] *Faretta v. California* established that

there is also a right to self-representation.[257]

The ruling in *Gideon* would not apply under the Confederate Constitution as

that was a State criminal case and as stated many times previously, the Confederate

Bill of Rights did not apply to the States. However, a Federal case may have

resulted in the Confederate Supreme Court requiring appointment of counsel in all

Federal criminal cases.

---

[253] 287 U.S. 45, 71 (1932).

[254] 316 U.S. 455, 472 (1942).

[255] 372 U.S. 335, 341-45 (1963).

[256] 466 U.S. 668, 686 (1984).

[257] 422 U.S. 806, 819 (1975).

(18)

> **In suits at common law, where the value in
> controversy shall exceed twenty dollars, the right of
> trial by jury shall be preserved; and no fact so tried
> by a jury shall be otherwise reexamined in any court
> of the *Confederacy*, than according to the rules of
> common law.**

The Union's Seventh Amendment:

> In Suits at common law, where the value in controversy
> shall exceed twenty dollars, the right of trial by jury shall
> be preserved, and no fact tried by a jury, shall be
> otherwise re-examined in any Court of the United States,
> than according to the rules of the common law.

This is one of the few provisions of the Bill of Rights the Supreme Court of

the United States declined to apply to the States.

(19)

> **Excessive bail shall not be required, nor excessive
> fines imposed, nor cruel and unusual punishments
> inflicted.**

The Union's Eighth Amendment:

> Excessive bail shall not be required, nor excessive fines
> imposed, nor cruel and unusual punishments inflicted.

Bail may be used to release a defendant on conditions to ensure that he

shows up for trial and to protect society and may be denied if neither can be guaranteed.[258] The Framers of the Eighth Amendment also wrote this provision against the background of Anglo-American history prohibiting excessive fines as historically fines often amounted to a total forfeiture of property.[259]

The Supreme Court of the United States uses the evolving standards of decency that mark the process of a maturing society rather than the standards of when the Eighth Amendment was written.[260] Under this standard capital Punishment is constitutional.[261] However, the Supreme Court has restricted capital punishment to murder cases, prohibiting it from rape-only cases.[262] The Court also restricted punishments of defendants who committed crimes as juveniles, finding that they cannot be executed[263] or sentenced to life with no meaningful opportunity for early release upon demonstration of maturity and reform.[264] Again, this clause in the Confederate Constitution only constrained Federal action, so even if the

---

[258] *United States v. Salerno*, 481 U.S. 739, 750-52 (1987).

[259] McDonald, *Novus Ordo Seclorum*, 21.

[260] *Gregg v. Georgia*, 428 U.S. 153, 172-73 (1976).

[261] *Id.* at 177.

[262] *Coker v. Georgia*, 433 U.S. 584, 600 (1977); *Kennedy v. Louisiana*, 554 U.S. 407, 413 (2008).

[263] *Roper v. Simmons*, 543 U.S. 551, 575 (2005).

[264] *Graham v. Florida*, 560 U.S. 48, 75 (2010); *Miller v. Alabama*, 567 U.S. 460, 479-80 (2012).

Confederate Supreme Court adopted the U.S. Supreme Court's interpretations of

cruel and unusual punishment, the individuals States could punish as they pleased.

(20)

> **Every law, or resolution having the force of law, shall**
> **relate to but one subject, and that shall be expressed**
> **in the title.**

This clause is original to the Confederate Constitution. One abuse of

procedure common in Congress is the rider, a bill that is not popular enough to

gain support to pass so it is attached to a popular or necessary bill to get it through.

For example, during the Obama Administration Republicans attached a rider to the

Credit Card Reform Bill allowing people to carry firearms in Federal parks.[265]

Often members of Congress use riders to get their pet projects through. The

Confederates eliminated this possibility by adopting a single-subject rule. As with

other clauses in the Confederate Constitution this would have helped keep the

budget balanced and prevent the passages of legislation the majority did not care

for. Some States have similar provisions today. For example, Florida's

Constitution requires laws to embrace only one subject: bills may include any

---

[265] Carl Hulse, "Bill Changing Credit Card Rules is Sent to Obama With Gun Measure Included," May 20, 2009: http://www.nytimes.com/2009/05/21/us/politics/21cards.html (accessed March 22, 2018).

matter properly connected to that subject and the subject must be briefly expressed in the title. [266]

Sec. 10.

(1)

> **No State shall enter into any treaty, alliance, or confederation; grant letters of marque and reprisal; coin money; make anything but gold and silver coin a tender in payment of debts; pass any bill of attainder, or ex post facto law, or law impairing the obligation of contracts; or grant any title of nobility.**

> No State shall enter into any Treaty, Alliance, or Confederation; grant Letters of Marque and Reprisal; coin Money; emit Bills of Credit; make any Thing but gold and silver Coin a Tender in Payment of Debts; pass any Bill of Attainder, ex post facto Law, or Law impairing the Obligation of Contracts, or grant any Title of Nobility.

Some of these provisions came from the Articles of Confederation.[267] The Confederates omitted the clause prohibiting States from emitting bills of credit. This clause was initially added because such bills rapidly depreciated.[268] The prohibition on States impairing contract obligations stems from the Confederation period after the Revolution where many States passed laws that effectively

---

[266] FLA. CONST. art. III, section 6; *Franklin v. State*, 887 So.2d 1063, 1072 (Fla. 2004).

[267] Articles of Confederation of 1781, art. VI.

[268] McDonald, *Novus Ordo Seclorum*, 27.

nullified contracts, allowing poor debtors evade payment to wealthy creditors.[269]

Chief Justice Marshall actively used this clause to invalidate State laws.[270] State

abuse in over-printing money in the days following the Revolution also contributed

to this section.[271]

(2)

> **No State shall, without the consent of the Congress, lay any imposts or duties on imports or exports, except what may be absolutely necessary for executing its inspection laws; and the net produce of all duties and imposts, laid by any State on imports, or exports, shall be for the use of the Treasury of the *Confederate* States; and all such laws shall be subject to the revision and control of Congress.**

> No State shall, without the Consent of the Congress, lay any Imposts or Duties on Imports or Exports, except what may be absolutely necessary for executing it's inspection Laws: and the net Produce of all Duties and Imposts, laid by any State on Imports or Exports, shall be for the Use of the Treasury of the United States; and all such Laws shall be subject to the Revision and Controul of the Congress.

This provision was designed to prevent the trade wars that plagued the States

prior to the adoption of the Constitution.

---

[269] Jackson, *Anti-Federalists*, 162.

[270] E.g. *Fletcher v. Peck*, 10 U.S. (6 Cranch) 87 (1810); *Dartmouth College v. Woodward*, 17 U.S. (4 Weat.) 518 (1819).

[271] *Id.*

(3)

> **No State shall, without the consent of Congress, lay any duty on tonnage,** *except on seagoing vessels, for the improvement of its rivers and harbors navigated by the said vessels; but such duties shall not conflict with any treaties of the Confederate States with foreign nations; and any surplus revenue thus derived shall, after making such improvement, be paid into the common treasury.* **Nor shall any State keep troops or ships of war in time of peace, enter into any agreement or compact with another State, or with a foreign power, or engage in war, unless actually invaded, or in such imminent danger as will not admit of delay.** *But when any river divides or flows through two or more States they may enter into compacts with each other to improve the navigation thereof.*

> No State shall, without the Consent of Congress, lay any Duty of Tonnage, keep Troops, or Ships of War in time of Peace, enter into any Agreement or Compact with another State, or with a foreign Power, or engage in War, unless actually invaded, or in such imminent Danger as will not admit of delay.

Many of these prohibitions already existed in some form under the Articles of Confederation.[272] The Confederates created exceptions to some of the provisions originally found in the United States Constitution. These exceptions pertained to taxes on vessels that passed through the waters of a particular State and allowed States to make agreements regarding shared rivers.

---

[272] Articles of Confederation of 1781, art. VI.

ARTICLE II

Section 1.

(1)

> **The executive power shall be vested in a President of the Confederate States of America. He and the Vice President shall hold their offices for the term of *six* years*; but the President shall not be reeligible*. The President and Vice President shall be elected as follows:**

The Union version of this section plus Section 1 of the Twenty-Second

Amendment:

> The executive Power shall be vested in a President of the United States of America. He shall hold his Office during the Term of four Years, and, together with the Vice President, chosen for the same Term, be elected, as follows
>
> No person shall be elected to the office of the President more than twice, and no person who has held the office of President, or acted as President, for more than two years of a term to which some other person was elected President shall be elected to the office of the President more than once. But this article shall not apply to any person holding the office of President when this article was proposed by the Congress, and shall not prevent any person who may be holding the office of President, or acting as President, during the term within which this article becomes operative from holding the office of President or acting as President during the remainder of such term.

The Anti-Federalists feared that the President would eventually become a

king, noting that many of the powers vested in the U.S. President were comparable

98

to those of the British monarch.[273] Hamilton answered these criticisms by noting that some of his powers, such as appointing government officers, are shared with the Senate.[274] He also noted that the British monarch was a hereditary life-time position rather than an elective one that serves for four years with fewer powers and can be removed from office.[275] The Anti-Federalists countered that because the President and Senate were dependent on each other they would work in concert with each other.[276]

The Confederates changed the terms of office of the President and Vice President from four years to six years. They also adopted term limits before the United States did in 1951.

During the drafting of the U.S. Constitution it was debated how long the President should serve. Some Founders such as Alexander Hamilton, despite his defense in the Federalist Papers, favored an executive that served for life unless he was removed from office or voluntarily stepped down.[277] The First Draft of the

---

[273] Patrick Henry, June 7, 1788.

[274] THE FEDERALIST NO. 67 (Alexander Hamilton).

[275] THE FEDERALIST NO. 69 (Alexander Hamilton).

[276] Cato VII, January 3, 1788.

[277] Alexander Hamilton, Plan for National Government, June 18, 1787.

Constitution gave the President a single, seven year term.[278] The debate focused on whether re-eligibility would make the President more or less prone to corruption. A President that can be reelected has motivation to perform well in office lest he be voted out, but he also has motivation to resort to corruption to try to engineer his own reelection.[279] Modern examples of the latter include the Watergate scandal of the 1972 election and the Hillary Clinton email investigation/James Comey/Loretta Lynch controversy of the 2016 election.

Ultimately the Philadelphia Convention decided on a term of four years with the possibility of reelection, originally for an unlimited number of terms. One Anti-Federalist concern about the lack of term-limits was that the President may abuse his power to engineer his reelection for as long as he wished.[280] Some people allege that this happened during the 1864 election.[281] The Confederates apparently found these arguments more persuasive and restricted their President to a single, six year term. Had the Confederacy survived Jefferson Davis would

---

[278] First draft U.S.CONST., art. X, section 1.

[279] Constitutional Convention, The National Executive, July 17, 19, 1787; Election and Powers of the President, September 7, 10, 15, 1787.

[280] Main, *The Anti-Federalists*, 140-41.

[281] Martin F. Graham, Clint Johnson, Richard A. Sauers, and George Skoch, *Blue and the Gray*, Plubications International, Ltd.: Lincolnwood, IL 2006, 230.

actually have served seven years as he got a one year term under the Confederacy's Provisional Constitution plus the six years of the permanent Constitution.

In the United States, after Franklin Delano Roosevelt's unprecedented election to four terms the Constitution was amended to allow a person to only be elected President twice unless that person served over two years of a term someone else was elected to in which case that person could only be elected once, a theoretical limit of ten years in office. This likely stemmed from Washington and Jefferson's decisions to not seek third terms, but it also is similar to an amendment proposed by the Virginian Ratification Convention that stated that no one should serve more than eight years as President within a term of sixteen years.[282]

(2)

> **Each State shall appoint, in such manner as the Legislature thereof may direct, a number of electors equal to the whole number of Senators and Representatives to which the State may be entitled in the Congress; but no Senator or Representative or person holding an office of trust or profit under the Confederate States shall be appointed an elector.**
>
> Each State shall appoint, in such Manner as the Legislature thereof may direct, a Number of Electors, equal to the whole Number of Senators and Representatives to which the State may be entitled in the Congress: but no Senator or Representative, or Person

---

[282] Amendments Proposed by the Virginia Convention: A Proposed Bill of Rights, June 27, 1788, http://avalon.law.yale.edu/18th_century/ratva.asp (accessed June 26, 2018).

holding an Office of Trust or Profit under the United
States, shall be appointed an Elector.

Hamilton defended the Electoral College by arguing that the President should be chosen by people with adequate information and discernment, something the average citizen was not likely to have.[283] It also tempered people's minds by avoiding violent movements to ensure one candidate's election over another.[284] Other defenses of the Electoral College include that it prevents heavily populated States from dominating the less populated States. Hamilton intended for the States to be divided into electoral districts, and the people of each district would elect and Elector.[285] He disliked the idea of pledged Electors. However, his plan was not incorporated into the original Constitution as the other Framers opted to give each State discretion in how to choose Electors. In early elections the State Legislatures chose Electors, but slowly every State adopted a popular vote scheme by which the candidate who won the popular vote in that State won all of the Electors for that State. Later Maine and Nebraska adopted a scheme by which the winner of the State-wide election won two Electors (representing the two Senators) and each candidate got one Elector for every Congressional District he or she won (representing the Representatives).

---

[283] THE FEDERALIST NO. 68 (Alexander Hamilton).

[284] *Id.*

[285] Alexander Hamilton, Plan for National Government, June 18, 1787.

(3)

The electors shall meet in their respective States and vote by ballot for President and Vice President, one of whom, at least, shall not be an inhabitant of the same State with themselves; they shall name in their ballots the person voted for as President, and in distinct ballots the person voted for as Vice President, and they shall make distinct lists of all persons voted for as President, and of all persons voted for as Vice President, and of the number of votes for each, which lists they shall sign and certify, and transmit, sealed, to the seat of the Government of. the Confederate States, directed to the President of the Senate; the President of the Senate shall, in the presence of the Senate and House of Representatives, open all the certificates, and the votes shall then be counted; the person having the greatest number of votes for President shall be the President, if such number be a majority of the whole number of electors appointed; and if no person have such majority, then from the persons having the highest numbers, not exceeding three, on the list of those voted for as President, the House of Representatives shall choose immediately, by ballot, the President. But in choosing the President the votes shall be taken by States, the representation from each State having one vote; a quorum for this purpose shall consist of a member or members from two-thirds of the States, and a majority of all the States shall be necessary to a choice. And if the House of Representatives shall not choose a President, whenever the right of choice shall devolve upon them, before the 4th day of March next following, then the Vice President shall act as President, as in case of the death, or other constitutional disability of the President.

(4)

The person having the greatest number of votes as Vice President shall be the Vice President, if such

number be a majority of the whole number of electors appointed; and if no person have a majority, then, from the two highest numbers on the list, the Senate shall choose the Vice President; a quorum for the purpose shall consist of two-thirds of the whole number of Senators, and a majority of the whole number shall be necessary to a choice.

(5)

But no person constitutionally ineligible to the office of President shall be eligible to that of Vice President of the *Confederate* States.

The Union version of original Article II, Section 3:

The Electors shall meet in their respective States, and vote by Ballot for two Persons, of whom one at least shall not be an Inhabitant of the same State with themselves. And they shall make a List of all the Persons voted for, and of the Number of Votes for each; which List they shall sign and certify, and transmit sealed to the Seat of the Government of the United States, directed to the President of the Senate. The President of the Senate shall, in the Presence of the Senate and House of Representatives, open all the Certificates, and the Votes shall then be counted. The Person having the greatest Number of Votes shall be the President, if such Number be a Majority of the whole Number of Electors appointed; and if there be more than one who have such Majority, and have an equal Number of Votes, then the House of Representatives shall immediately chuse by Ballot one of them for President; and if no Person have a Majority, then from the five highest on the List the said House shall in like Manner chuse the President. But in chusing the President, the Votes shall be taken by States, the Representation from each State having one Vote; A quorum for this Purpose shall consist of a Member or Members from two thirds of the States, and a Majority of all the States shall be necessary to a Choice. In every

Case, after the Choice of the President, the Person having the greatest Number of Votes of the Electors shall be the Vice President. But if there should remain two or more who have equal Votes, the Senate shall chuse from them by Ballot the Vice President.

Twelfth Amendment to the United States Constitution:

The Electors shall meet in their respective states, and vote by ballot for President and Vice-President, one of whom, at least, shall not be an inhabitant of the same state with themselves; they shall name in their ballots the person voted for as President, and in distinct ballots the person voted for as Vice-President, and they shall make distinct lists of all persons voted for as President, and of all persons voted for as Vice-President, and of the number of votes for each, which lists they shall sign and certify, and transmit sealed to the seat of the government of the United States, directed to the President of the Senate;—The President of the Senate shall, in the presence of the Senate and House of Representatives, open all the certificates and the votes shall then be counted;—The person having the greatest number of votes for President, shall be the President, if such number be a majority of the whole number of Electors appointed; and if no person have such majority, then from the persons having the highest numbers not exceeding three on the list of those voted for as President, the House of Representatives shall choose immediately, by ballot, the President. But in choosing the President, the votes shall be taken by states, the representation from each state having one vote; a quorum for this purpose shall consist of a member or members from two-thirds of the states, and a majority of all the states shall be necessary to a choice. And if the House of Representatives shall not choose a President whenever the right of choice shall devolve upon them, before the fourth day of March next following, then the Vice-President shall act as President, as in the case of the death or other constitutional disability of the President. —The person having the greatest number of votes as Vice-President, shall be the Vice-President, if such number be a majority of the whole number of Electors appointed, and if no person have a majority, then from the two highest numbers on the list, the Senate shall choose the Vice-President; a quorum for the purpose shall consist of two-thirds of the whole number of Senators, and a majority of the whole number shall be necessary to a choice. But no person constitutionally ineligible to the office of President shall be eligible to that of Vice-President of the United States.

The original scheme of the U.S. Constitution declared that Presidential Electors got two votes and the Vice President was the second-place winner of the Presidential race. However, the Framers did not anticipate the role that political parties would play in elections. In the election of 1800 both the Federalist and Democratic-Republican Parties, each party not wanting the other to hold any office, put up two candidates for President with the understanding that one of the Presidential Electors would throw away his second vote enabling the primary candidate to become President with his running mate becoming Vice President. Unfortunately the one Democratic-Republican Elector with that responsibility neglected to do so resulting in a tie between Thomas Jefferson and his running mate Aaron Burr. The Twelfth Amendment fixed this problem, and the Confederates wrote the Twelfth Amendment directly into their Article II.

Curiously, the deadline for choosing the President in the event of a House runoff election is March 4 in both Constitutions despite that date being the Union's original Inauguration Day while the Confederate Inauguration Day was February

22. The U.S. Constitution was subsequently amended again to change this date.

The Twentieth Amendment reads in part:

> Section 1: Each State shall appoint, in such Manner as the Legislature thereof may direct, a Number of Electors, equal to the whole Number of Senators and Representatives to which the State may be entitled in the Congress: but no Senator or Representative, or Person holding an Office of Trust or Profit under the United States, shall be appointed an Elector.

> Section 3: If, at the time fixed for the beginning of the term of the President, the President elect shall have died, the Vice President elect shall become President. If a President shall not have been chosen before the time fixed for the beginning of his term, or if the President elect shall have failed to qualify, then the Vice President elect shall act as President until a President shall have qualified; and the Congress may by law provide for the case wherein neither a President elect nor a Vice President elect shall have qualified, declaring who shall then act as President, or the manner in which one who is to act shall be selected, and such person shall act accordingly until a President or Vice President shall have qualified.

> Section 4: The Congress may by law provide for the case of the death of any of the persons from whom the House of Representatives may choose a President whenever the right of choice shall have devolved upon them, and for the case of the death of any of the persons from whom the Senate may choose a Vice President whenever the right of choice shall have devolved upon them.

(6)

The Congress may determine the time of choosing the electors, and the day on which they shall give their

votes; which day shall be the same throughout the *Confederate* States.

The Congress may determine the Time of chusing the Electors, and the Day on which they shall give their Votes; which Day shall be the same throughout the United States.

(7)

No person except a natural-born citizen of the *Confederate* States, or a citizen *thereof* at the time of the adoption of this Constitution, *or a citizen thereof born in the United States prior to the 20th of December, 1860,* shall be eligible to the office of President; neither shall any person be eligible to that office who shall not have attained the age of thirty-five years, and been fourteen years a *resident within the limits of the Confederate States, as they may exist at the time of his election.*

No Person except a natural born Citizen, or a Citizen of the United States, at the time of the Adoption of this Constitution, shall be eligible to the Office of President; neither shall any Person be eligible to that Office who shall not have attained to the Age of thirty five Years, and been fourteen Years a Resident within the United States.

As with the qualifications for the House and Senate, the citizenship and residency requirements of the Confederacy were adjusted for its young age.

(8)

In case of the removal of the President from office, or of his death, resignation, or inability to discharge the powers and duties of said office, the same shall devolve on the Vice President; and the Congress may, by law, provide for the case of removal, death,

resignation, or inability, both of the President and Vice President, declaring what officer shall then act as President; and such officer shall act accordingly until the disability be removed or a President shall be elected.

In Case of the Removal of the President from Office, or of his Death, Resignation, or Inability to discharge the Powers and Duties of the said Office, the Same shall devolve on the Vice President, and the Congress may by Law provide for the Case of Removal, Death, Resignation or Inability, both of the President and Vice President, declaring what Officer shall then act as President, and such Officer shall act accordingly, until the Disability be removed, or a President shall be elected.

One issue with this clause is that under the original U.S. Constitution and the Confederate Constitution it is unclear if "the same" that devolves on the Vice President refers to the "powers and duties of said office" or the "office" itself. Did the Framers intend for the Vice President to become President should the sitting President die, resign, or be removed from office or was he merely "Acting President"? When Union President William Henry Harrison died his Vice President John Tyler used the language from Article I, Section 3 "unless [the Vice President] shall exercise the Office of President of the United States" to declare that he actually became the President. The problem with Tyler's reading is that under Article II the Vice President also "exercises" the office in the event of the President's temporary disability.

The Confederate Constitution

For purposes of the Union Constitution there was no practical difference between a Vice President becoming Acting President or actually becoming the President as he would have the same authority either way. However, this issue would be troublesome for the Confederates given that the President was ineligible for reelection. A Confederate Vice President would likely want to reject the Tyler Precedent, styling himself "Acting President" so that he could later run for election to a full term as President. The United States eventually codified the Tyler Precedent and established procedures regarding Presidential disability in the Twenty-Fifth Amendment:

> 1: In case of the removal of the President from office or of his death or resignation, the Vice President shall become President.
>
> 2: Whenever there is a vacancy in the office of the Vice President, the President shall nominate a Vice President who shall take office upon confirmation by a majority vote of both Houses of Congress.
>
> 3: Whenever the President transmits to the President pro tempore of the Senate and the Speaker of the House of Representatives his written declaration that he is unable to discharge the powers and duties of his office, and until he transmits to them a written declaration to the contrary, such powers and duties shall be discharged by the Vice President as Acting President.
>
> 4: Whenever the Vice President and a majority of either the principal officers of the executive departments or of such other body as Congress may by law provide, transmit to the President pro tempore of the Senate and the Speaker of the House of Representatives their written

declaration that the President is unable to discharge the powers and duties of his office, the Vice President shall immediately assume the powers and duties of the office as Acting President.

Thereafter, when the President transmits to the President pro tempore of the Senate and the Speaker of the House of Representatives his written declaration that no inability exists, he shall resume the powers and duties of his office unless the Vice President and a majority of either the principal officers of the executive department or of such other body as Congress may by law provide, transmit within four days to the President pro tempore of the Senate and the Speaker of the House of Representatives their written declaration that the President is unable to discharge the powers and duties of his office. Thereupon Congress shall decide the issue, assembling within forty-eight hours for that purpose if not in session. If the Congress, within twenty-one days after receipt of the latter written declaration, or, if Congress is not in session, within twenty-one days after Congress is required to assemble, determines by two-thirds vote of both Houses that the President is unable to discharge the powers and duties of his office, the Vice President shall continue to discharge the same as Acting President; otherwise, the President shall resume the powers and duties of his office.

(9)

The President shall, at stated times, receive for his services a compensation, which shall neither be increased nor diminished during the period for which he shall have been elected; and he shall not receive within that period any other emolument from the *Confederate* States, or any of them.

The President shall, at stated Times, receive for his Services, a Compensation, which shall neither be encreased nor diminished during the Period for which he

111

shall have been elected, and he shall not receive within that Period any other Emolument from the United States, or any of them.

This provision prevented Congress from trying to undermine or bribe the President.[286] George Washington initially refused his salary and had to be persuaded to take it. Some Presidential candidates try to win popularity by doing the same. For example, Donald Trump once stated that he would take one dollar as his salary,[287] though he ultimately donated the first quarter of his salary to the Department of Veterans' Affairs.[288]

(10)

> **Before he enters on the execution of his office he shall take the following oath or affirmation: "I do solemnly swear (or affirm) that I will faithfully execute the office of President of the *Confederate* States, and will, to the best of my ability, preserve, protect, and defend the Constitution *thereof*.**

> Before he enter on the Execution of his Office, he shall take the following Oath or Affirmation:—"I do solemnly swear (or affirm) that I will faithfully execute the Office of President of the United States, and will to the best of

---

[286] THE FEDERALIST NO. 73 (Alexander Hamilton).

[287] "How common is Trump's $1 salary?," BBC, November 14, 2016. https://www.bbc.com/news/election-us-2016-37977433 (accessed June 18, 2018).

[288] Amy Sherman, "Trump donates first-quarter salary to VA," Politifact, May 18, 2018. http://www.politifact.com/truth-o-meter/promises/trumpometer/promise/1341/take-no-salary/ (accessed June 18, 2018).

my Ability, preserve, protect and defend the Constitution of the United States."

Zachary Taylor started his Presidency a day late because he refused to take this oath on a Sunday. A humorous issue surrounding this clause was when Barack Obama was sworn in both he and Chief Justice John Roberts tried to recite the oath from memory, resulting in the two fumbling the wording.[289] To avoid a controversy that Obama was not properly sworn in the oath was re-administered in a private ceremony.[290]

Sec. 2.

(1)

> **The President shall be Commander-in-Chief of the Army and Navy of the *Confederate* States, and of the militia of the several States, when called into the actual service of the *Confederate* States; he may require the opinion, in writing, of the principal officer in each of the Executive Departments, upon any subject relating to the duties of their respective offices; and he shall have power to grant reprieves and pardons for offenses against the *Confederate* States, except in cases of impeachment.**

> 1: The President shall be Commander in Chief of the Army and Navy of the United States, and of the Militia of the several States, when called into the actual Service

---

[289] Samuel P. Jacobs, "After fumbled oath, Roberts and Obama leave little to chance," Reuters, January 18, 2013. https://www.reuters.com/article/us-usa-inauguration-roberts/after-fumbled-oath-roberts-and-obama-leave-little-to-chance-idUSBRE90H16L20130118 (accessed June 18, 2018).

[290] *Id.*

of the United States; he may require the Opinion, in
writing, of the principal Officer in each of the executive
Departments, upon any Subject relating to the Duties of
their respective Offices, and he shall have Power to grant
Reprieves and Pardons for Offences against the United
States, except in Cases of Impeachment.

Hamilton argued that these powers were necessary to direct the government's full strength in one direction during emergencies such as war.[291] Since the creation of the Presidency Americans debated how far the President's Commander in Chief powers extend. Some politicians, including notably then Representative Abraham Lincoln, criticized President Polk for starting the Mexican-American War by sending troops to what he claimed the U.S.-Mexico border was.[292] Polk knew or should have known that this territory was disputed and that by doing so he would likely provoke a war. As President Lincoln did something similar at the start of the Civil War, keeping troops in Fort Sumter and sending relief supplies knowing it would provoke a Confederate attack. Both Lincoln and Davis pushed their Commander in Chief powers to the limit during the Civil War. Lincoln controversially did so to issue the Emancipation Proclamation despite claims that such a proclamation went beyond his authority.

---

[291] THE FEDERALIST NO. 74 (Alexander Hamilton).

[292] "Lincoln's Spot Resolutions," National Archives, September 7, 2016, https://www.archives.gov/education/lessons/lincoln-resolutions (accessed July 18, 2018).

The Supreme Court later adopted in *Dames & Moore v. Regan* (in reliance

on Justice Robert Jackson's concurrence in *Youngstown Sheet & Tube Co. v.*

Sawyer[293]) a tripartite test to determine if the President was acting constitutionally:

the President's power is at its greatest when he is acting pursuant to Congressional

authorization, if Congress is silent on the issue he may be in a zone of ambiguity of

whether Congress or the President has certain authority, and finally the President's

power is at its lowest when Congress prohibits him from doing something in which

the President may only succeed if the Supreme Court invalidates the act of

Congress.[294]

While the Anti-Federalists opposed the President's pardoning power, fearing

that he would use it to screen violators of civil liberties from punishment,[295] the

Confederates retained it. Alexander Hamilton defended the pardon as it is

sometimes necessary to ensure justice.[296] Both Lincoln and Davis used this power

to grant clemency to convicted deserters during the Civil War. Some later

Presidential pardons were controversial, such as when Gerald R. Ford pardoned

former President Richard Nixon, George H.W. Bush pardoning Regan-era officials

---

[293] 343 U.S. 579 (1952).

[294] 453 U.S. 654, 668-69 (1981).

[295] "Centinel" Number 1 (October 5, 1787); Pennsylvania Minority
(December 18, 1787).

[296] THE FEDERALIST NO. 74 (Alexander Hamilton).

involved in the Iran-Contra affair, Clinton's pardoning 140 people on his last day in office, and Donald Trump's pardon of Joe Arpaio.

(2)

> **He shall have power, by and with the advice and consent of the Senate, to make treaties; provided two-thirds of the Senators present concur; and he shall nominate, and by and with the advice and consent of the Senate shall appoint, ambassadors, other public ministers and consuls, judges of the Supreme Court, and all other officers of the *Confederate* States whose appointments are not herein otherwise provided for, and which shall be established by law; but the Congress may, by law, vest the appointment of such inferior officers, as they think proper, in the President alone, in the courts of law, or in the heads of departments.**

> He shall have Power, by and with the Advice and Consent of the Senate, to make Treaties, provided two thirds of the Senators present concur; and he shall nominate, and by and with the Advice and Consent of the Senate, shall appoint Ambassadors, other public Ministers and Consuls, Judges of the supreme Court, and all other Officers of the United States, whose Appointments are not herein otherwise provided for, and which shall be established by Law: but the Congress may by Law vest the Appointment of such inferior Officers, as they think proper, in the President alone, in the Courts of Law, or in the Heads of Departments.

The Federalists supported a national treaty power as they believed that a single national government was preferable for treaty stability than thirteen individual States and that such a power was necessary to avoid war with foreign nations.[297] A strong nation also has the power to exact favorable treaty terms for all of its members than a small nation would.[298] This particular arrangement existed to ensure that treaties were crafted by most qualified men and in a manner most conductive to the public good.[299] Hamilton defended the requirement of consent by two-thirds present rather than two-thirds membership to avoid Senators from manipulating the process by their absence.[300] Thomas Jefferson used the treaty power to justify the Louisiana Purchase which was otherwise unauthorized by the U.S. Constitution.[301]

(3)

> **The principal officer in each of the Executive Departments, and all persons connected with the diplomatic service, may be removed from office at the pleasure of the President. All other civil officers of the Executive Departments may be removed at any time by the President, or other appointing power, when their services are unnecessary, or for dishonesty, incapacity, inefficiency, misconduct, or neglect of duty; and when so removed, the removal shall be reported to the Senate, together with the reasons therefor.**

---

[297] THE FEDERALIST No. 3 (John Jay).

[298] *Id.*

[299] THE FEDERALIST NO. 63 (John Jay).

[300] THE FEDERALIST NO. 75 (Alexander Hamilton).

[301] McDonald, *Novus Ordo Seclorum*, 283.

This section was original to the Confederate Constitution. It codified what many believed was already implicit in the Constitution. The Constitution provides for the appointment of Executive officers and their removal via the impeachment process, but it does not say whether or not the President can fire them at will. Andrew Jackson fired members of his Cabinet for not obeying his orders.[302]

After the Civil War the Union faced a controversy of whether Congress could restrain this removal power. Because Andrew Johnson wanted to dismiss Secretary of War Edwin Stanton Congress passed, over Johnson's veto, the Tenure of Office Act of 1867 to prevent Johnson from doing so. Johnson removed Stanton anyway, so the House of Representatives impeached him. Part of Johnson's defense in his Senate trial was that the Tenure of Office Act was unconstitutional. Johnson was acquitted by a single vote. Later in *Myers v. United States* the Supreme Court found a similar law unconstitutional and noted in dicta that Johnson was correct that the Tenure of Office Act was unconstitutional.[303] However, this absolute removal power does not extend to independent agencies

---

[302] Gutzman, *The Politically Incorrect Guide to the Constitution*, 106.

[303] 272 U.S. 52, 176 (1926).

created by Congress; Congress can limit the removal of the heads of those

agencies.[304]

Under the Confederate version the Tenure of Office Act would be outright

unconstitutional. However, the Confederate Constitution limited the President's

ability to relieve other civil officers of duty.

(4)

> **The President shall have power to fill all vacancies that may happen during the recess of the Senate, by granting commissions which shall expire at the end of their next session;** *but no person rejected by the Senate shall be reappointed to the same office during their ensuing recess.*

> 3: The President shall have Power to fill up all Vacancies that may happen during the Recess of the Senate, by granting Commissions which shall expire at the End of their next Session.

The recess appointment is another controversial aspect of the Presidency.

While designed to keep government offices in operation in the event of a vacancy

during a Senate recess, sometimes the Senate rejects a Presidential nominee, so the

President waits until the next recess to make the appointment. The Confederates

closed this loophole.

Because such language is not in the Union Constitution the Union Congress

crafted a different solution. The Senate now will often hold pro forma sessions to

---

[304] *Free Enterprise Fund v. Public Co. Accounting Oversight Bd.*, 561 U.S. 477, 478-79 (2010).

prevent a recess thus blocking recess appointments. President Obama declared that gaps between pro forma sessions were recesses in which he could make an appointment, but the Supreme Court unanimously rejected this argument in *N.L.R.B. v. Noel Canning*.[305]

Sec. 3.

(1)

> **The President shall, from time to time, give to the Congress information of the state of the *Confederacy*, and recommend to their consideration such measures as he shall judge necessary and expedient; he may, on extraordinary occasions, convene both Houses, or either of them; and in case of disagreement between them, with respect to the time of adjournment, he may adjourn them to such time as he shall think proper; he shall receive ambassadors and other public ministers; he shall take care that the laws be faithfully executed, and shall commission all the officers of the *Confederate* States.**

> He shall from time to time give to the Congress Information of the State of the Union, and recommend to their Consideration such Measures as he shall judge necessary and expedient; he may, on extraordinary Occasions, convene both Houses, or either of them, and in Case of Disagreement between them, with Respect to the Time of Adjournment, he may adjourn them to such Time as he shall think proper; he shall receive Ambassadors and other public Ministers; he shall take Care that the Laws be faithfully executed, and shall Commission all the Officers of the United States.

---

[305] 134 S.Ct. 2550, 2573-74 (2014).

This clause is the origin of the traditional State of the Union Address.

Originally the President simply transmitted a written annual message to Congress.

Woodrow Wilson changed this custom by making a public speech before a joint

session of Congress every year, and every President has followed it since.

Sec. 4.

(1)

> **The President, Vice President, and all civil officers of the *Confederate* States, shall be removed from office on impeachment for and conviction of treason, bribery, or other high crimes and misdemeanors.**

> The President, Vice President and all civil Officers of the United States, shall be removed from Office on Impeachment for, and Conviction of, Treason, Bribery, or other high Crimes and Misdemeanors.

Because a high crime or misdemeanor refers to a crime committed by a

public official, presumably one can only be impeached for crimes committed in

office, not those committed before taking office. Some argue that this clause

should be read narrowly. For example, one defense of Bill Clinton regarding his

impeachment was that his alleged perjury involved a personal matter, not an

official act as President.[306] Others argue that this phrase should be read more

---

[306] "The Impeachment of Bill Clinton," Bill of Rights Institute, 2018, https://billofrightsinstitute.org/educate/educator-resources/lessons-plans/presidents-constitution/clinton-impeachment/ (accessed June 18, 2018).

broadly, including even non-indictable offenses such as drunkenness on duty, maladministration, and even judges misapplying the law.[307]

---

[307] Gutzman, *The Politically Incorrect Guide to the Constitution*, 77-81.

ARTICLE III

Section I.

(1)

> **The judicial power of the *Confederate* States shall be vested in one Supreme Court, and in such inferior courts as the Congress may, from time to time, ordain and establish. The judges, both of the Supreme and inferior courts, shall hold their offices during good behavior, and shall, at stated times, receive for their services a compensation which shall not be diminished during their continuance in office.**

> The judicial Power of the United States, shall be vested in one supreme Court, and in such inferior Courts as the Congress may from time to time ordain and establish. The Judges, both of the supreme and inferior Courts, shall hold their Offices during good Behaviour, and shall, at stated Times, receive for their Services, a Compensation, which shall not be diminished during their Continuance in Office.

The basic structure of Article III was from the Virginia Plan.[308] The Supreme Court was created to ensure the uniformity of all major legal determinations.[309] Hamilton defended the tenure of "good behavior" or rather life unless impeached or voluntarily stepping down as necessary to isolate judges from corruption.[310] He further noted that the judiciary has control over neither the sword

---

[308] Edmund Randolph, "The Virginia Plan," May 29, 1787.

[309] THE FEDERALIST NO. 22 (Alexander Hamilton).

[310] THE FEDERALIST NO. 78-79 (Alexander Hamilton).\

nor the purse, so it depends entirely on the executive branch to enforce its judgments.[311] This was reflected in Andrew Jackson's apocryphal quote, "John Marshal has made his ruling, now let him enforce it." Despite these protections the Anti-Federalists still had misgivings about the Supreme Court as there was no means of correcting its errors, particularly those where the Court sided with the Federal government over the States.[312] They thought that the Court and Congress would collude to empower Congress to legislate on any subject.[313] The Confederate government never created a Supreme Court, but it did create inferior courts, usually appointing former United States judges to Confederate judgeships correlating to their Union counterparts.

Sec. 2.

(1)

> **The judicial power shall extend to all cases arising under this Constitution, the laws of the *Confederate* States, and treaties made, or which shall be made, under their authority; to all cases affecting ambassadors, other public ministers and consuls; to all cases of admiralty and maritime jurisdiction; to controversies to which the *Confederate* States shall be a party; to controversies between two or more States; between a State and citizens of another State, *where***

---

[311] THE FEDERALIST NO. 78 (Alexander Hamilton).

[312] Brutus XI, January 31, 1788.

[313] Main, *The Anti-Federalists*, 125.

> ***the State is plaintiff*; between citizens claiming lands under grants of different States; and between a State or the citizens thereof, and foreign states, citizens, or subjects; *but no State shall be sued by a citizen or subject of any foreign state.***

The original Union version:

> The judicial Power shall extend to all Cases, in Law and Equity, arising under this Constitution, the Laws of the United States, and Treaties made, or which shall be made, under their Authority;—to all Cases affecting Ambassadors, other public Ministers and Consuls;—to all Cases of admiralty and maritime Jurisdiction;—to Controversies to which the United States shall be a Party;—to Controversies between two or more States;—between a State and Citizens of another State;—between Citizens of different States, —between Citizens of the same State claiming Lands under Grants of different States, and between a State, or the Citizens thereof, and foreign States, Citizens or Subjects.

The Eleventh Amendment to the U.S. Constitution modified this section:

> The Judicial power of the United States shall not be construed to extend to any suit in law or equity, commenced or prosecuted against one of the United States by Citizens of another State, or by Citizens or Subjects of any Foreign State.

As held in *Chisholm, Ex'r v. Georgia*[314] the original version of the U.S. Constitution allowed States to be sued by citizens of other States. The Eleventh Amendment was passed to repudiate this decision. The Confederates incorporated this amendment into their Article III.

---

[314] 2 U.S. 419, 425 (1793).

The Confederate Constitution

The Confederates also eliminated diversity jurisdiction for the Federal courts, requiring people to sue out-of-State citizens in the courts of the defendant's home State. The Framers of the U.S. Constitution feared that the out-of-State plaintiffs would be at a disadvantage in another State's courts,[315] but apparently the Confederates had no such fear. This omission is similar to a proposed Anti-Federalist amendment to the Constitution by Virginia's Ratification convention.[316] Massachusetts proposed a different measure that would have eliminated diversity jurisdiction from the Federal judiciary with the exception of property disputes valued at least $1,500, and the Supreme judiciary would not gain jurisdiction unless that amount was at least $3,000.[317] Currently, the U.S. Congress uses its regulatory ability to limit diversity jurisdiction to cases valued in excess of $75,000.[318]

One issue that arose from this subsection is the cases or controversies requirement. In 1793 President George Washington sought an advisory opinion as

---

[315] Joseph W. Gannon, Andrew M. Perlman, and Peter Raven-Hansen, *Civil Procedure: A Coursebook*, Walters Kluwer Law & Business: New York, NY 2011, 14-15.

[316] Amendments Proposed by the Virginia Convention: A Proposed Bill of Rights, June 27, 1788.

[317] Amendments Proposed by the Massachusetts Convention, February 27, 1787, http://avalon.law.yale.edu/18th_century/ratma.asp (accessed June 26, 2018).

[318] 28 U.S.C. § 1332(b).

to legal questions on America's neutrality during the French Revolution Wars.[319]

The Justices informed Washington that they cannot give such opinions as they can only rule on existing cases and controversies.[320] Additionally, plaintiffs bringing action in Federal court must have an injury that is personal to them that is causally connected to the conduct complained of and the injury is likely and not merely speculative.[321] Individuals seeking relief in Federal court must have a personal stake in the outcome in order to have standing to bring suit.[322]

Judicial jurisdiction is also limited by the mootness doctrine which declares that the Court will not hear cases if situation that brought about the suit no longer exists, but an exception to this rule is when the case is capable of repetition yet evading review (such as election and abortion related cases).[323] The ripeness doctrine requires that some actual harm occur before filing suit, barring premature claims.[324] For example, in *Laird v. Tatum* the Court rejected a challenge to an Army surveillance of political activity program as the Army had not yet misused

---

[319] Sullivan and Gunther, *Constitutional Law*, 31.

[320] *Id.*

[321] *Lujan v. Defenders of Wildlife*, 504 U.S. 555, 560-61 (1992).

[322] *Baker v. Carr*, 369 U.S. 204 (1962).

[323] Sullivan and Gunther, *Constitutional Law*, 47-48.

[324] *Id.* at 48.

such information.[325] The Court cannot use its power to address purely political

questions.[326]

(2)

> **In all cases affecting ambassadors, other public
> ministers and consuls, and those in which a State shall
> be a party, the Supreme Court shall have original
> jurisdiction. In all the other cases before mentioned,
> the Supreme Court shall have appellate jurisdiction
> both as to law and fact, with such exceptions and
> under such regulations as the Congress shall make.**

> In all Cases affecting Ambassadors, other public
> Ministers and Consuls, and those in which a State shall
> be Party, the supreme Court shall have original
> Jurisdiction. In all the other Cases before mentioned, the
> supreme Court shall have appellate Jurisdiction, both as
> to Law and Fact, with such Exceptions, and under such
> Regulations as the Congress shall make.

The landmark *Marbury v. Madison*[327] case that elaborated on judicial review

in the Union ruled on this section. The Supreme Court found that Congress

unconstitutionally extended the Court's grant of original jurisdiction.[328]

(3)

> **The trial of all crimes, except in cases of
> impeachment, shall be by jury, and such trial shall be**

---

[325] 408 U.S. 1, 13 (1972).

[326] 5 U.S. 137, 166 (1803).

[327] 5 U.S. 137.

[328] *Id.* at 176.

held in the State where the said crimes shall have been committed; but when not committed within any State, the trial shall be at such place or places as the Congress may by law have directed.

The Trial of all Crimes, except in Cases of Impeachment, shall be by Jury; and such Trial shall be held in the State where the said Crimes shall have been committed; but when not committed within any State, the Trial shall be at such Place or Places as the Congress may by Law have directed.

The requirement that crimes be tried in the State in which they were committed stems from an abuse of the British government during the Colonial era where Colonists accused of crimes against the Crown were transported to Great Britain for trial rather than being tried in the Colony where the crime was allegedly committed.[329]

Sec. 3.

(1)

Treason against the *Confederate* States shall consist only in levying war against them, or in adhering to their enemies, giving them aid and comfort. No person shall be convicted of treason unless on the testimony of two witnesses to the same overt act, or on confession in open court.

Treason against the United States, shall consist only in levying War against them, or in adhering to their Enemies, giving them Aid and Comfort. No Person shall be convicted of Treason unless on the Testimony of two

---

[329] THE DECLARATION OF INDEPENDENCE para. 20 (U.S. 1776).

> Witnesses to the same overt Act, or on Confession in
> open Court.

The Union Framers limited the definition of treason as various sessions of Parliament throughout British history constantly broadened the definition of treason and treason carried a strong stigma in Anglo-American thought. The Supreme Court ruled in *Cramer v. United States* that merely harboring disloyal sympathies is not enough to constitute treason.[330] There must be some act of aid and comfort to the enemy.[331] Even acts that may indirectly help the enemy, such as criticizing the government, profiteering, or striking in factories do not constitute treason.[332] The Framers also required direct evidence, as opposed to circumstantial evidence, to prove treason in court: the testimony of two witnesses or a confession in open court.[333] While adherence to the enemy cannot be proven by direct evidence (witnesses cannot read the mind of the accused), the overt act of treason can and the intent must be proven from that overt act.[334] For an overt act to be

---

[330] 325 U.S. 1, 29 (1945).

[331] *Id.*

[332] *Id.*

[333] *Id.* at 30.

[334] *Id.* at 31.

considered treason the witnesses must testify to sufficient action by the accused in its setting to show that he or she actually gave aid and comfort to the enemy.[335]

Following the Civil War many Confederate leaders such as Jefferson Davis were indicted for treason, but they were never brought to trial and the charges were eventually dismissed. As the Court noted in *Cramer* proving treason is incredibly difficult under this clause as there must be two witnesses to the "over act" or a "confession in open court." The only witnesses to high ranking Confederates' "treason" would be other Confederates. Union prosecutors would have had to convince the former Confederates to turn on each other to secure convictions for treason.

(2)

> **The Congress shall have power to declare the punishment of treason; but no attainder of treason shall work corruption of blood, or forfeiture, except during the life of the person attainted.**
>
> The Congress shall have Power to declare the Punishment of Treason, but no Attainder of Treason shall work Corruption of Blood, or Forfeiture except during the Life of the Person attainted.

Under prior English law when one was convicted of treason the whole family suffered. Usually this came in the form of confiscation of family land and titles. "Corruption of Blood" refers to other legal consequences on the family of

---

[335] *Id.* at 34.

the convicted traitor.[336] For example, when King Edward IV's brother George,

Duke of Clarence was convicted of treason not only was he executed but his

children were removed from the line of succession.

---

[336] McDonald, *Novus Ordo Seclorum*, 20.

ARTICLE IV

Section I.

(1)

> **Full faith and credit shall be given in each State to the public acts, records, and judicial proceedings of every other State; and the Congress may, by general laws, prescribe the manner in which such acts, records, and proceedings shall be proved, and the effect thereof.**

> Full Faith and Credit shall be given in each State to the public Acts, Records, and judicial Proceedings of every other State. And the Congress may by general Laws prescribe the Manner in which such Acts, Records and Proceedings shall be proved, and the Effect thereof.

Article IV of the United States and Confederate Constitutions is largely a carry-over from Article IV of the Articles of Confederation with modifications.[337]

Sec. 2.

(1)

> **The citizens of each State shall be entitled to all the privileges and immunities of citizens in the several States; *and shall have the right of transit and sojourn in any State of this Confederacy, with their slaves and other property; and the right of property in said slaves shall not be thereby impaired.***

> The Citizens of each State shall be entitled to all Privileges and Immunities of Citizens in the several States.

---

[337] Articles of Confederation of 1781, art. IV.

The Confederates added a clause to this section clarifying a constitutional

dispute that arose under the U.S. Constitution: whether or not travelers and visitors

from slave States could bring their slaves into free soil States. In early U.S. history

many free soil States extended courtesy protection of slavery to traveling and

visiting slave owners. Likewise, such traveling slaveholders usually did not

complain when a State refused to recognize their slavery rights as it was their own

fault for bringing their slaves to a free State.

However, as the Compromise of 1850 unraveled, both sides lost the ability

to work with each other. Free States insisted that once a slave was voluntarily

brought into their territory by the slave's owner, the slave became a free man or

woman. Southerners began claiming that the Constitution gave them a right to

travel anywhere in the United States with their slaves. This latter claim fueled the

North's belief in the slave power conspiracy, the fear that some in the South

wanted all of America as slave soil.

This issue also came to the forefront in the *Dred Scott* case because Dred

Scott was brought by his master to Illinois.[338] Prior precedent of the Supreme

Court of Missouri, Scott's home State, held that he became free once he crossed

the State line, but in Scott's case the Missouri Supreme Court reversed its prior

holding and ruled that by returning to Missouri he reaccepted his condition as a

---

[338] 60 U.S. 393, 397.

slave.[339] The U.S. Supreme Court did not address the issue of traveling slaves-owners, but many including Lincoln feared that the *Dred Scott* holding would pave the way for Southerners transporting slaves throughout the country.

The Confederate Constitution resolved this controversy in favor of slaveholders, but States in the Confederacy still had the right to abolish slavery within their borders, prohibiting the permanent settlement of slaves. Some Confederate Framers considered requiring all States to be slave States, but this was rejected in hopes that some mid-western States would join the Confederacy.

(2)

> **A person charged in any State with treason, felony, or other crime *against the laws of such State*, who shall flee from justice, and be found in another State, shall, on demand of the executive authority of the State from which he fled, be delivered up, to be removed to the State having jurisdiction of the crime.**

> A Person charged in any State with Treason, Felony, or other Crime, who shall flee from Justice, and be found in another State, shall on Demand of the executive Authority of the State from which he fled, be delivered up, to be removed to the State having Jurisdiction of the Crime.

A fugitive from justice is one who is charged with a crime that happened while he or she was bodily present in that State but subsequently left the State.[340]

---

[339] *Id.* at 452-53.

[340] *Appleyard v. Massachusetts*, 203 U.S. 222, 226 (1906).

It does not matter the reason why an individual left the State or what knowledge the accused had of pending prosecution.[341]

Originally, in *Commonwealth of Kentucky v. Dennison* the Supreme Court ruled that a writ of mandamus could not be used to compel one State governor to extradite a person to another State that demanded such extradition.[342] This effectively gave State governors the de facto power to refuse extradition. However, the Court reversed this prior holding in *Puerto Rico v. Branstad*, ruling that Federal courts can compel State governors to order extradition.[343]

(3)

> **No *slave or other person* held to service or labor in *any* State *or Territory of the Confederate States*, under the laws thereof, escaping *or lawfully carried* into another, shall, in consequence of any law or regulation therein, be discharged from such service or labor; but shall be delivered up on claim of the party to whom *such slave belongs, or to whom* such service or labor may be due.**

> No Person held to Service or Labour in one State, under the Laws thereof, escaping into another, shall, in Consequence of any Law or Regulation therein, be discharged from such Service or Labour, but shall be delivered up on Claim of the Party to whom such Service or Labour may be due.

---

[341] *Bassing v. Cady*, 208 U.S. 386, 394 (1908).
[342] 65 U.S. 66, 77-79 (1860).

[343] 483 U.S. 219, 227-29 (1987).

The Union version was the result of the arguments of John Rutledge, Union Framer and later U.S. Supreme Court justice.[344] The Confederate Constitution clarifies that this clause applies to the territories as well as the States. It also adds a clause to reference lawful transportation of slaves across State lines pursuant to the changes in the previous subsection.

Sec. 3.

(1)

> ***Other States* may be admitted into this *Confederacy by a vote of two-thirds of the whole House of Representatives and two-thirds of the Senate, the Senate voting by States*; but no new State shall be formed or erected within the jurisdiction of any other State, nor any State be formed by the junction of two or more States, or parts of States, without the consent of the Legislatures of the States concerned, as well as of the Congress.**

> New States may be admitted by the Congress into this Union; but no new State shall be formed or erected within the Jurisdiction of any other State; nor any State be formed by the Junction of two or more States, or Parts of States, without the Consent of the Legislatures of the States concerned as well as of the Congress.

The Union Constitution improved upon the Articles of Confederation by clarifying whether or not new States could enter the Union beyond Canada and

---

[344] Gutzman, *The Politically Incorrect Guide to the Constitution*, 114.

other British colonies.[345] One controversy under this clause was the admission of Texas which unlike other States was not previously a territory of the United States or part of a preexisting State but rather was an independent nation for nine years prior to joining the Union. Another was the creation of West Virginia as the government of Virginia did not consent to its separation as this clause requires.[346] Lincoln argued that the loyalist government of West Virginia was the government of Virginia thus could consent to its creation. However, this argument is tenuous as the official government of Virginia was still in operation even if its people were "in rebellion against the United States." After the Civil War Virginia gave its consent to avoid further controversy.

The Confederacy made it more difficult to admit new States by requiring a two-third vote in each House with the Senate voting by State. This was similar to the First Draft of the U.S. Constitution which required a two-third vote in each House of Congress, but the Senate did not have to vote by State.[347] Perhaps the Confederate Framers wanted to guarantee that newly admitted States held the same values as a super-majority of the Confederate States. Otherwise the disputes that

---

[345] THE FEDERALIST NO. 43 (James Maddison).

[346] Gutzman, *The Politically Incorrect Guide to the Constitution*, 128.

[347] First draft U.S.CONST., preamble.

led to the dissolution of the Union might repeat themselves as the Confederacy would have become politically too diverse.

(2)

> **The Congress shall have power to dispose of and make all needful rules and regulations concerning the property of the *Confederate* States, *including the lands thereof*.**
>
> The Congress shall have Power to dispose of and make all needful Rules and Regulations respecting the Territory or other Property belonging to the United States; and nothing in this Constitution shall be so construed as to Prejudice any Claims of the United States, or of any particular State.

The Union Framers added this section to prevent strife over what to do with territory the United States won from Great Britain during the Revolution.[348] The Confederates restricted the language of this section, likely with the *Dred Scott* decision in mind where the Supreme Court of the United States ruled that this section of the Union Constitution did not empower Congress to enact general legislation on the territories, only organize territorial governments.[349] This interpretation went against the desire of that clause's author Gouverneur Morris

---

[348] THE FEDERALIST NO. 7 (Alexander Hamilton).

[349] 60 U.S. 393, 339-40.

who hoped that newly acquired territory would never be admitted as States, wanting such territories to be controlled perpetually as provinces.[350]

(3)

> **The Confederate States may acquire new territory; and Congress shall have power to legislate and provide governments for the inhabitants of all territory belonging to the Confederate States, lying without the limits of the several Sates; and may permit them, at such times, and in such manner as it may by law provide, to form States to be admitted into the Confederacy. In all such territory the institution of negro slavery, as it now exists in the Confederate States, shall be recognized and protected be Congress and by the Territorial government; and the inhabitants of the several Confederate States and Territories shall have the right to take to such Territory any slaves lawfully held by them in any of the States or Territories of the Confederate States.**

This subsection was original to the Confederate Constitution. First, it clarified that the Confederacy could in fact acquire new territory. During the Jefferson Administration many people, including Jefferson himself, questioned the validity of the Louisiana Purchase, noting that the U.S. Constitution did not explicitly authorized the Federal government to acquire territory.[351] The Supreme Court later ruled that the Federal government can acquire territory through treaty

---

[350] McDonald, *Novus Ordo Seclourm*, 282-83.

[351] John Buchanan, *Jackson's Way: Andrew Jackson and the People of the Western Waters*, John Wiley & Sons, Inc.: New York, NY 2001, 172.

or conquest.[352] The Confederates rejected a portion of *Dred Scott* that ruled that this clause only applied to territory already owned at the time the Constitution was adopted.[353] The next clause of this subsection codified a portion of *Dred Scott* holding that the Federal government had the power to organize territorial governments for the inhabitants of the territories.[354]

The Confederate Constitution also resolved the question of whether or not slavery should exist in the territories, the biggest issue of the 1860 Presidential election, in favor of slavery. This section confirmed the holding in the *Dred Scott* case that the U.S. Constitution prior to the Thirteenth Amendment protected the right to bring into and hold slaves in the territories of the United States.[355] Abraham Lincoln ran for President on a campaign to overturn this ruling, and his election sparked the secession of seven Southern States, and four more followed in response to Lincoln's call for troops.

(4)

> **The *Confederate* States shall guarantee to every State**
> ***that now is, or hereafter may become, a member of this***
> ***Confederacy,* a republican form of government; and**

---

[352] *American Ins. Co. v. 356 Bales of Cotton*, 26 U.S. 511, 511 (1828).

[353] 60 U.S. 393, 339-40.

[354] 60 U.S. 393, 447-48.

[355] *Id.* at 450.

shall protect each of them against invasion; and on application of the Legislature or of the Executive (when the Legislature is not in session) against domestic violence.

The United States shall guarantee to every State in this Union a Republican Form of Government, and shall protect each of them against Invasion; and on Application of the Legislature, or of the Executive (when the Legislature cannot be convened) against domestic Violence.

After the American Revolution, most Americans, unlike their British counterparts, had participated in government in some manner, so they came to regard a republican form of government to be the best for the preservation of liberty.[356] Maddison stated that this provision was necessary to ensure that aristocratic and monarchist elements did not seep into the American government while the protections against invasion and domestic violence are protections typically expected of the government.[357] However, different Founders had different definitions of what constituted a republic. Hamilton defined it as one where no one had a hereditary status.[358] Maddison, a slave holder, defined it as one where the government derived its consent from the "public."[359]

---

[356] McDonald, *Novus Ordo Seclorum*, 1.

[357] THE FEDERALIST NO. 43 (James Maddison).

[358] *Id.* at 5.

[359] *Id.*

The Confederate Constitution

The clause in the U.S. Constitution guaranteeing the States a republican form of government was sometimes cited in support of Congress' Reconstruction policies following the Civil War.

ARTICLE V

Section I.

(1)

Upon the demand of any three States, legally assembled in their several conventions, the Congress shall summon a convention of all the States, to take into consideration such amendments to the Constitution as the said States shall concur in suggesting at the time when the said demand is made; and should any of the proposed amendments to the Constitution be agreed on by the said convention, voting by States, and the same be ratified by the Legislatures of two- thirds of the several States, or by conventions in two-thirds thereof, as the one or the other mode of ratification may be proposed by the general convention, they shall thenceforward form a part of this Constitution. But no State shall, without its consent, be deprived of its equal representation in the Senate.

The Congress, whenever two thirds of both Houses shall deem it necessary, shall propose Amendments to this Constitution, or, on the Application of the Legislatures of two thirds of the several States, shall call a Convention for proposing Amendments, which, in either Case, shall be valid to all Intents and Purposes, as Part of this Constitution, when ratified by the Legislatures of three fourths of the several States, or by Conventions in three fourths thereof, as the one or the other Mode of Ratification may be proposed by the Congress; Provided that no Amendment which may be made prior to the Year One thousand eight hundred and eight shall in any Manner affect the first and fourth Clauses in the Ninth Section of the first Article; and that no State, without its Consent, shall be deprived of its equal Suffrage in the Senate.

The Confederate Constitution

The Articles of Confederation required unanimous consent for an amendment to pass because each State was sovereign thus a change to Articles affecting ever State required the consent of every State.[360] The Framers of the Union Constitution altered this requirement to strike a balance between having a Constitution too susceptible to change and one that is almost impossible to change.[361] States were to retain equal representation in the Senate as a residual of their sovereignty.[362]

The Confederate Framers drastically changed the method for amending the Constitution. They eliminated the power of Congress to propose Constitutional Amendments. However, they made it somewhat easier for States to call for Constitutional Conventions by only requiring three States to summon such a convention rather than two-thirds as under the U.S. Constitution. However, those three States had to act pursuant to a State constitutional convention demanding an amendment, not by an act of the State Legislatures. This requirement would have resulted in the people of the Confederacy being directly involved in the amendment process to some extent, thus any change to the Constitution would have been the product of "the people of the Confederate States."

---

[360] Gutzman, *The Politically Incorrect Guide to the Constitution*, 13-14.

[361] THE FEDERALIST NO. 43.

[362] *Id.*

Ratification of a proposed amendment was easier as the number of States required to ratify an amendment was reduced from three-fourths to two-thirds. This answered a concern of some Anti-Federalists that amending the Constitution was too difficult which could in turn prevent the passage of necessary amendments such as the Bill of Rights.[363] The national convention rather than Congress decided whether ratification is to be done by State Legislatures or by State constitutional conventions.

One clarification that the Confederate Article V made is what a national convention may consider. Under the United States Constitution it is presently debated whether an Article V convention may only be summoned for a particular purpose or if the entire Constitution is open to revision once a convention is summoned. The Confederate Constitution states that such conventions may only consider issues agreed upon by the three States that summoned the convention. This provision answered one criticism of the Philadelphia Convention: it was summoned only for the purpose of revising the Articles of Confederation but instead proposed a new Constitution.[364] Maddison defended the Convention's actions as it was summoned to frame, "a *national government*, adequate to the

---

[363] "John DeWitt II," October 27, 1787.

[364] Wills, Introduction to *The Federalist Papers*, vii.

exigencies of government and *of the Union.*"[365] The Confederates ensured that a

future convention would not exceed its mandate.

---

[365] THE FEDERALIST NO. 40.

ARTICLE VI

I.

> **The Government established by this Constitution is the successor of the Provisional Government of the Confederate States of America, and all the laws passed by the latter shall continue in force until the same shall be repealed or modified; and all the officers appointed by the same shall remain in office until their successors are appointed and qualified, or the offices abolished.**

This section is original to the Confederate Constitution. It established greater continuity with the predecessor government of the Confederacy. The United States had less of an established government under the Articles of Confederation thus did not need such a section.

2.

> **All debts contracted and engagements entered into before the adoption of this Constitution shall be as valid against the *Confederate* States under this Constitution, as under the *Provisional Government*.**

> 1: All Debts contracted and Engagements entered into, before the Adoption of this Constitution, shall be as valid against the United States under this Constitution, as under the Confederation.

This section in both Constitutions deals with the relationship between the new governments and their constitutional predecessors.

3.

> **This Constitution, and the laws of the *Confederate* States made in pursuance thereof, and all treaties made, or which shall be made, under the authority of the *Confederate* States, shall be the supreme law of the land; and the judges in every State shall be bound thereby, anything in the constitution or laws of any State to the contrary notwithstanding.**

> 2: This Constitution, and the Laws of the United States which shall be made in Pursuance thereof; and all Treaties made, or which shall be made, under the Authority of the United States, shall be the supreme Law of the Land; and the Judges in every State shall be bound thereby, any Thing in the Constitution or Laws of any State to the Contrary notwithstanding.

The phrase "supreme Law of the Land" was adopted over the proposed "supreme law of the several States" (similar to language from the New Jersey Plan[366]) to imply that judges were to use the Constitution to determine the validity of both national and State law.[367] The Anti-Federalists saw this clause as proof that the Constitution created nothing less than a consolidation of the States into a single, general government.[368] Hamilton defended this clause as self-evident: "A LAW by the very meaning of the term includes supremacy."[369] He stated that only

---

[366] "The New Jersey Plan," June 15, 1787.

[367] McDonald, *Novus Ordo Seclorum*, 255.

[368] "Centinel" Number 1 (October 5, 1787).

[369] THE FEDERALIST NO. 33 (Alexander Hamilton).

laws passed "in Pursuance" of the Constitution were part of the Supreme law of the land.[370] The courts are to void laws that were not passed "in Pursuance" of the Constitution.[371] The first time the Supreme Court struck down a Federal law was in *Marbury v. Maddison* and the second time was in *Dred Scott v. Sandford*.[372]

Despite being a more States' rights friendly Constitution, the Confederates retained the controversial Supremacy Clause that gives the Federal Constitution and statutes precedent over State constitutions and statutes. James Maddison defended this clause as necessary to prevent States from annulling Federal law and to enable the United States to maintain diplomacy with foreign nations without individual States violating treaties thus making the United States' word meaningless.[373] Anti-Federalists feared that this clause would nullify State constitutions and laws.[374]

4.

The Senators and Representatives before mentioned, and the members of the several State Legislatures, and all executive and judicial officers, both of the

---

[370] *Id.*

[371] THE FEDERALIST NO. 78 (Alexander Hamilton).

[372] McDonald, *Novus Ordo Seclorum*, 276.

[373] THE FEDERALIST NO. 44 (James Maddison).

[374] Brutus I, October 18, 1787.

Confederate **States and of the several States, shall be bound by oath or affirmation to support this Constitution; but no religious test shall ever be required as a qualification to any office or public trust under the** *Confederate* **States.**

3: The Senators and Representatives before mentioned, and the Members of the several State Legislatures, and all executive and judicial Officers, both of the United States and of the several States, shall be bound by Oath or Affirmation, to support this Constitution; but no religious Test shall ever be required as a Qualification to any Office or public Trust under the United States.

The various government officials, State and Federal, were required to take an oath supporting the Constitution as their services were necessary to give the Constitution effect.[375]

The Test Clause had its origin in 17th Century English and early Colonial laws excluding Catholics and other religious dissenters from holding office by requiring them to take oaths denouncing key tenets of their faith.[376] In the context of military chaplains the Confederates put the ban on religious tests into practice before the Union did. When the Confederate Army was established Congress only required that chaplains be ordained members of the clergy without specifying a

---

[375] THE FEDERALIST NO. 44 (James Maddison).

[376] McDonald, *Novus Ordo Seclorum*, 42.

particular religious sect.[377] Originally the United States only allowed Protestant ministers to become chaplains.[378] During the Mexican-American War Catholic chaplains were allowed to serve as well.[379] It was not until 1862 that Jewish rabbis were allowed to become chaplains in the U.S. Army.[380] However, this did not stop Lieutenant General Ulysses S. Grant from expelling Jews from the Department of Tennessee.[381] The Confederate population likewise had its fair share of Anti-Semitism.[382] It should also be noted that the first two Jews in the U.S. Senate came from Southern States: David Levy Yulee of Florida and Judah P. Benjamin of Louisiana (who later held several Confederate cabinet positions).[383]

5.

> **The enumeration, in the Constitution, of certain rights shall not be construed to deny or disparage others retained by the people of the several States.**

---

[377] Bertram Wallace Korn, *American Jewry and the American Civil War*, The Jewish Publication Society of America: Philadelphia, PA 1951, 57.

[378] *Id.* at 56.

[379] *Id.*

[380] *Id.* at 71-72.

[381] *Id.* at 122-23.

[382] *Id.* at 175-76.

[383] *Id.* at 16, 172-73.

The Ninth Amendment to the United States Constitution:

> The enumeration in the Constitution, of certain rights,
> shall not be construed to deny or disparage others
> retained by the people.

Originally many Framers of the Constitution opposed a Bill of Rights.
Because the Federal government could only exercise the powers delegated to it, a
Bill of Rights was seen as unnecessary as the Federal government was not
empowered to infringe on certain rights.[384] Some Founders even thought it
dangerous to include a Bill of Rights as listing some rights might leave the
implication that other rights were not protected, and the Framers might overlook an
important right.[385] The Ninth Amendment was adopted as a catch-all to ensure that
any right traditionally recognized by Anglo-American society would be protected
from a more expansive reading of Congress' powers. Secessionists could also look
to the Ninth Amendment for the right to overthrow their government, a right
referenced in the Declaration of Independence[386] but not the Constitution.

6.

> **The powers not delegated to the *Confederate* States by
> the Constitution, nor prohibited by it to the States,**

---

[384] McDonald, *Novus Ordo Seclorum*, 269.

[385] THE FEDERALIST NO. 84 (Alexander Hamilton).

[386] THE DECLARATION OF INDEPENDENCE para. 2 (U.S. 1776).

> **are reserved to the States, respectively, or to the**
> **people thereof.**

The Tenth Amendment to the United States Constitution:

> The powers not delegated to the United States by the
> Constitution, nor prohibited by it to the States, are
> reserved to the States respectively, or to the people.

The Tenth Amendment was the linchpin of the secessionists' arguments in the events leading up to the Civil War. They declared that nothing in the Constitution empowers the Federal government to prohibit a State from seceding nor does the Constitution expressly prohibit the States from doing so.[387] Therefore, States must have the right to secede.[388] Because the Confederate Constitution reads the same, theoretically the States of the Confederacy could one day have seceded from the Confederacy. Georgia threatened to do so during the Civil War in response to Jefferson Davis' wartime policies.

Chief Justice Marshall downplayed the Tenth Amendment in the U.S. Constitution, noting that while the Articles of Confederation read, "Each state retains…every power, jurisdiction, and right, which is not by this Confederation

---

[387] Davis, *The Rise and Fall of the Confederate Government*, 145.

[388] *Id.*

expressly delegated to the United States, in Congress assembled,"[389] the Tenth

Amendment omits the word "expressly."[390] The Supreme Court later declared that,

> The amendment states but a truism that all is retained
> which has not been surrendered. There is nothing in the
> history of its adoption to suggest that it was more than
> declaratory of the relationship between the national and
> state governments as it had been established by the
> Constitution before the amendment.[391]

Arguably Chief Justice Marshall forgot this logic when he relied on the omission

of the word "expressly" as even Alexander Hamilton admitted that under the pre-

Tenth Amendment Constitution, "the State Governments would clearly retain all

the rights of sovereignty which they before had and which were not by that act

exclusively delegated to the United States."[392]

---

[389] Articles of Confederation of 1781, art. II.

[390] 17 U.S. 316, 384.

[391] *Darby*, 312 U.S. 100, 124.

[392] THE FEDERALIST NO. 32. (Alexander Hamilton).

ARTICLE VII

1.

> **The ratification of the conventions of *five* States shall
> be sufficient for the establishment of this Constitution
> between the States so ratifying the same.**
>
> The Ratification of the Conventions of nine States, shall
> be sufficient for the Establishment of this Constitution
> between the States so ratifying the Same.

James Maddison supported sending the Constitution to ratifying conventions chosen by the people rather than the State Legislatures because otherwise the Constitution would be seen as purely an agreement among the States and thus a violation by one State would release the others from their obligations.[393] By contrast other Federalists such as George Nicholas at the Virginia Ratification Convention argued that the United States was still a compact under the Constitution.[394]

Opponents of the Constitution criticized this article as it circumvented the Articles of Confederation's unanimity requirement for amending the Articles of Confederation.[395] By only requiring nine States to ratify the Constitution for it to

---

[393] "Method of Ratification," July 23, 1787; THE FEDERALIST NO. 43 (James Maddison); McDonald, *Novus Ordo Seclorum*, 279-80.

[394] Gutzman, *The Politically Incorrect Guide to the Constitution*, 37.

[395] Wills, Introduction to *The Federalist Papers*, vii; "Debate on the New Jersey Plan," June 16, 1787.

take effect such ratification would put unfair pressure on the last four States to ratify or be excluded from the Union.[396] Maddison countered that twelve of the States containing most of the United States' population may want a particular change but a single, stubborn State with a small population can block an essential change.[397] Having fewer member States the Confederacy required fewer States to ratify the Constitution for it to become effective.

Secessionists used this article to support the right of the State to secede.[398] They noted that the Constitution was binding only on States that agreed to be bound to it. They reasoned that if the Constitution can be ratified, it can also be de-ratified. When Virginia, New York, and Rhode Island ratified that Constitution they specifically declared that the people retained the power to take back the powers delegated to the Federal government.[399] South Carolina's Ordinance of Secession even read,

---

[396] Patrick Henry, June 7, 1788; Wills, Introduction to *The Federalist Papers*, vii.

[397] THE FEDERALIST NO. 40 and 43 (James Maddison)1.

[398] Davis, *The Rise and Fall of the Confederate Government*, 92.

[399] Ratification of the Constitution by the State of Virginia; June 26, 1788, http://avalon.law.yale.edu/18th_century/ratva.asp (accessed April 4, 2018); Ratification of the Constitution by the State of New York; July 26, 1788, http://avalon.law.yale.edu/18th_century/ratny.asp (accessed April 4, 2018);

> We, the people of the State of South Carolina, in
> convention assembled, do declare and ordain, and it is
> hereby declared and ordained, That the ordinance
> adopted by us in convention on the twenty-third day of
> May, in the year of our Lord one thousand seven hundred
> and eighty-eight, whereby the Constitution of the United
> States of America was ratified, and also all acts and parts
> of acts of the General Assembly of this State ratifying
> amendments of the said Constitution, are hereby
> repealed; and that the union now subsisting between
> South Carolina and other States, under the name of the
> "United States of America," is hereby dissolved.[400]

Jefferson Davis noted that during the first year of the U.S. Constitution's operation

North Carolina and Rhode Island had not ratified the Constitution and were treated

as independent nations by the Washington Administration until they did.[401]

2.

> **When five States shall have ratified this Constitution,
> in the manner before specified, the Congress under
> the Provisional Constitution shall prescribe the time
> for holding the election of President and Vice
> President; and for the meeting of the Electoral
> College; and for counting the votes, and inaugurating
> the President. They shall, also, prescribe the time for
> holding the first election of members of Congress
> under this Constitution, and the time for assembling
> the same. Until the assembling of such Congress, the**

Ratification of the Constitution by the State of Rhode Island; May 29, 1790,
http://avalon.law.yale.edu/18th_century/ratri.asp (accessed April 4, 2018).

[400] South Carolina Ordinance of Secession (December 20, 1861).
https://web.archive.org/web/20040404171724/http://members.aol.com/jfepperson/
ordnces.html (accessed April 16, 2018).

[401] Davis, *The Rise and Fall of the Confederate Government*, 95.

Congress under the Provisional Constitution shall continue to exercise the legislative powers granted them; not extending beyond the time limited by the Constitution of the Provisional Government.

Unlike the United States Constitution, the Confederates added a section for the Constitution's actual implementation. The Confederation Congress provided a similar function for the United States Constitution as outlined in this section.

Signatures

Confederate

Adopted unanimously by the Congress of the Confederate States of South Carolina, Georgia, Florida, Alabama, Mississippi, Louisiana, and Texas, sitting in convention at the capitol, the city of Montgomery, Ala., on the eleventh day of March, in the year eighteen hundred and Sixty-one.

HOWELL COBB, President of the Congress.

South Carolina: R. Barnwell Rhett, C. G. Memminger, Wm. Porcher Miles, James Chesnut, Jr., R. W. Barnwell, William W. Boyce, Lawrence M. Keitt, T. J. Withers.

Georgia: Francis S. Bartow, Martin J. Crawford, Benjamin H. Hill, Thos. R. R. Cobb.

Florida: Jackson Morton, J. Patton Anderson, Jas. B. Owens.

Alabama: Richard W. Walker, Robt. H. Smith, Colin J. McRae, William P. Chilton, Stephen F. Hale, David P. Lewis, Tho. Fearn, Jno. Gill Shorter, J. L. M. Curry.

Mississippi: Alex. M. Clayton, James T. Harrison, William S. Barry, W. S. Wilson, Walker Brooke, W. P. Harris, J. A. P. Campbell.

Louisiana: Alex. de Clouet, C. M. Conrad, Duncan F. Kenner, Henry Marshall.

Texas: John Hemphill, Thomas N. Waul, John H. Reagan, Williamson S. Oldham,

Louis T. Wigfall, John Gregg, William Beck Ochiltree.

Union

Go: Washington -Presidt. and deputy from Virginia

Delaware
Geo: ReadGunning Bedford junJohn Dickinson
Richard Bassett
Jaco: Broom

Maryland
James McHenry
Dan of St   Thos. Jenifer
Danl Carroll.

Virginia
John Blair—
James Madison Jr.

North Carolina
Wm Blount
Richd. Dobbs Spaight.
Hu Williamson

South Carolina
J. Rutledge
Charles Cotesworth Pinckney
Charles Pinckney
Pierce Butler.

Georgia
William Few
Abr Baldwin

New Hampshire
John Langdon
Nicholas Gilman

Massachusetts
Nathaniel Gorham
Rufus King

Connecticut
Wm. Saml. Johnson
Roger Sherman

New York
Alexander Hamilton

New Jersey
Wil. Livingston
David Brearley.
Wm. Paterson.
Jona: Dayton

Pennsylvania
B Franklin
Thomas Mifflin
Robt Morris
Geo. Clymer
Thos. FitzSimons
Jared Ingersoll
James Wilson.
Gouv Morris

Afterward

Categories of the Changes Made

Most of the significant changes made in the Confederate Constitution fall into one or more of five categories:

1. Answering Anti-Federalist criticisms of the U.S. Constitution: e.g. directly invoking God, various provisions for promoting fiscal responsibility in government (line item veto, limiting spending powers of Congress, etc.) thus limiting debt and taxation to pay off that debt, restricting implied powers, term limits for the President, and limiting Congress' ability to set elections thus preventing Congress from expanding its own terms of office.

2. Resolving Constitutional disputes experienced under the U.S. Constitution: e.g. rejecting protective tariffs, rejecting Federally funded internal improvements, making the postal system self-funding, confirming the power of the Federal government to acquire territory, determining what powers Congress has over the territory, clarifying that slavery was protected in the territories, and clarifying whether or not slave holders could travel through free soil States.

3. Increasing States' Rights: e.g. more constrained wording delegating fewer powers to Congress, States gained the ability to impeach Federal officials,

and States could levy taxes related to waterways and make compacts relating to said waterways.

4. Limiting States' Rights: e.g. States could no longer extend the franchise to non-citizens or prohibit slaves from moving through their borders.

5. Confirming or expanding slavery rights: e.g. clarifying that slavery was protected in the territories, giving slave-holders the right to travel and sojourn throughout the Confederacy, confirming that Congress could not prohibit slavery, and referring to slavery by name rather than by euphemism.

What is Missing from the Confederate Constitution?

Because the Confederacy only lasted four years, three under its permanent Constitution, it is unknown what amendments it would have adopted for its Federal Constitution had it survived. Given the inability of Congress to propose an amendment perhaps it would not have been amended at all and all societal changes such as the inevitable abolition of slavery would have been accomplished at the State level. On the other hand, by requiring fewer States to call a convention and a smaller percentage of States to ratify perhaps it would have been amended several times.

The first of the U.S. Constitutional amendments to come out of the Civil War was the abolition of slavery. The subsequent Fourteenth Amendment granted citizenship to the former slaves and forbade States from denying people equal protection of the law. Without some equivalent of this amendment the Confederates would have to resolve citizenship questions in the Confederate Supreme Court. Various Supreme Court decisions on equal protection such as *Brown v. Board of Education*[402] (prohibiting school segregation) and *Obergefell v. Hodges*[403] (legalizing same-sex marriage nationwide) would not have happened in the Confederacy. Such changes could only be implemented by the State governments themselves. Also, as stated earlier in this book the Fourteenth Amendment was used by the Supreme Court to apply most of the Bill of Rights to the States. The States of the Confederacy would only be bound by their State bills of rights. The Due Process Clause of the Fourteenth Amendment was also used by the Supreme Court to create "un-enumerated rights" such as the right to privacy which has been used to protect access to contraceptives,[404] abortion,[405] and sodomy.[406]

As for voting rights, the Fifteenth, Nineteenth, and Twenty-Fourth, and Twenty-Sixth Amendments to the U.S. Constitution prohibited States from

---

[402] 347 U.S. 483 (1954).

[403] 576 U.S. ___ (2015).

[404] *Griswold*, 381 U.S. 479.

[405] *Roe v. Wade*, 410 U.S. 113 (1973).

[406] *Lawrence v. Texas*, 539 U.S. 558 (2003).

denying the right to vote based on race, color, previous condition of servitude, sex, failure to pay a poll tax, and age for those at least eighteen years old. The Confederate Constitution had no such protections. Each State could decide its own voting requirements except that all voters had to be Confederate citizens.

Finally, there were some structural changes to the U.S. government, such as succession to the Presidency, the start of the terms of office, the income tax, and the direct election of Senators that were implemented after the Civil War. The Confederate Constitution maintained the Union Founders' original formulas on these issues. On many of these issues there are merits to retaining those original formulas, such as having Senators elected by the State Legislatures who would presumably be more responsive to the needs of their entire States rather than the most populous regions of them.

Advantages of the Confederate Constitution

As stated throughout this book, the Confederate Constitution addressed several Anti-Federalist criticisms of the United States Constitution that the Bill of Rights failed to address. For example, the taxing and spending powers of the Confederate government were much more limited than their Union counterparts. The President's line item veto would enable him to do what Congress seems incapable of doing: balancing the budget. Given current debates over the national debt perhaps such limitations are necessary. Today we also see disputes over

The Confederate Constitution

Federal funding and its use to compel States to adhere to certain policies (drinking age, sanctuary cities, etc.). Under the Confederate model such Federal funding would be expressly unconstitutional, resulting in lower Federal taxes. States would then be able to pay for their own functions and adopted their own policies without Federal interference.

Given the greater limitations on Federal power, States' rights were afforded greater protection of their rights. While the Confederacy retained the Supremacy Clause, the powers of the Federal government were more restricted, reserving more power to the States. States also gained the ability to impeach Federal officials that operated exclusively within their borders. This would provide an additional layer of protection against corruption and Federal usurpation of States' rights.

Another advantage of the Confederate Constitution is that it took many of the major constitutional controversies of the preceding seven decades and provided definitive answers. For example, the Confederate Constitution expressly stated that the Federal government could acquire territory but it could not levy a protective tariff or finance most internal improvements, all three of which were matters of controversy in the 1800s.

Finally, with the Bill of Rights inapplicable to the States, State governments would have more leeway to be what the U.S. Supreme Court has called, "laboratories for devising solutions to difficult legal problems."[407] Different

people have different understanding of what rights should and should not be

protect, so the States could adjust their constitutions accordingly. Additionally,

many people criticize decisions of the U.S. Supreme Court which may be good

public policy but are not part of the Constitution's text thus beyond the scope of

the Court's power to implement.[408] In the Confederacy various issues surrounding

religious liberty, free speech, gun rights, privacy, crime and punishment, etcetera

would all be resolved by the State governments without Federal interference. If a

conservative State wanted to allow guns but ban abortion it could do so. If a

liberal State wanted to allow abortion but ban guns it could do it. Individuals who

do not like their current State's laws can "vote with their feet" and relocate to a

different State.

Another advantage to not binding the States by the Federal Bills of Rights is

that it may encourage State governments to offer more protection as they may be

encouraged to interpret their bills of rights more broadly than the Federal courts do

---

[407] *Arizona State Legislature v. Arizona Independent Redistricting Com'n*, 135 S.Ct. 2652, 2673 (2015).

[408] E.g. Justice Robert H. Jackson remarked that, "This Court is forever adding new stories to the temples of constitutional law, and the temples have a way of collapsing when one story too many is added…The Court is adding a new privilege to override the rights of others…In so doing it needlessly creates a risk of discrediting a wise provision of our Constitution…" *Douglas v. Jeannette*, 319 U.S. 157, 181-82 (1943)(Jackson, J. concurring).

Federal rights. Presently, the Federal Bill of Rights sets a floor of what States have to follow, but they can go above and beyond the Federal minimum. However, some States decide that the Federal minimum protection is also the State maximum. For example, the Supreme Court of Florida initially interpreted Florida's protection against unreasonable searches and seizures more broadly than its Federal counterpart.[409] Lawmakers and prosecutors did not like this arrangement so they amended the Florida Constitution to include a conformity clause binding its interpretation to U.S. Supreme Court interpretations of the Federal Fourth Amendment.[410] Without the incorporation doctrine, perhaps the people of Florida would have left their State Constitution alone, leaving the Florida courts free to interpret State constitutional protections independently and perhaps more broadly in favor of liberty than its Federal counterpart.

Disadvantages of the Confederate Constitution

The primary drawback of the Confederate Constitution is that it resolved every slavery-related debate from the 1800s in favor of slavery. While it maintained the Union's prohibition on the international slave trade and allowed States to still choose between being slave or free, the Confederacy required States to tolerate traveling and sojourning slave owners. It also clarified that slavery

---

[409] *Grubbs v. State*, 373 So.2d 905, 909 (Fla. 1979).

[410] FLA. CONST. art. I, section 12; *Soca v. State*, 673 So.2d 24, 26-27 (Fla. 1996).

would be protected in any newly acquired territory until such a time as that territory became a State. Only then could the people of the new State choose between being a slave of free State. However, it should be noted that this provision did nothing other than maintain the status quo. It did not increase the number of slaves actually existing in the Union or Confederacy. Until the Confederacy acquired territory (and it did claim to admit two territories from the United States, Arizona and the Indian Territory, which until 1862 were open to slavery under U.S. law) the provision protecting slavery in the territories would have had no practical use. Additionally, the American West was not suitable for a plantation style economy, thus slavery was already economically barred from the West, making the debate of slavery in the territory pointless. Had the South won the Civil War, or if the South had stayed in the Union, slavery would have continued in the South for a time and likely would have ultimately collapsed under its own weight.

A second drawback is that with the Bill of Rights inapplicable to the States, some States might offer less protection of personal liberty than they presently do. For example, States might still be denying attorneys to the criminally indigent or engaging in prosecutorial misconduct to obtain convictions. States might not require police to read suspects their *Miranda*[411] rights.

---

[411] 384 U.S. 436 (1966).

Other than these provisions most of the various changes to the Confederate Constitution would only be regarded as disadvantages to those who favor a large Federal government. As noted before, the Confederate Constitution either eliminated express grants of power given to the Confederate government or amended clauses to avoid broader readings of granted powers.

Conclusion

The Confederate Constitution provided for a more limited form of government than the United States Constitution. While some of its provisions are a dark reminder of the South's past and its attempts to preserve the 1860 status quo, other provisions are well worth considering. Had the Confederacy survived, it quite possibly would have enjoyed a more efficient, less indebted government than what presently governs the United States. Under the Confederate system people would have greater ability to pass laws to their liking without fear of having those laws voided by the Federal government. Regarding personal rights, States in the Confederacy would not be bound by the Federal model which might encourage some States to go above and beyond what the Federal system protects, but other States may offer less protection. However, the ability to travel to other States would remedy problems such as this.

Which Constitution is better? That is up to the reader to decide.

Appendix A: The Articles of Confederation and Perpetual Union

To all to whom these Presents shall come, we the undersigned Delegates of the States affixed to our Names send greeting.

Articles of Confederation and perpetual Union between the states of New Hampshire, Massachusetts-bay Rhode Island and Providence Plantations, Connecticut, New York, New Jersey, Pennsylvania, Delaware, Maryland, Virginia, North Carolina, South Carolina and Georgia.

I.

The Stile of this Confederacy shall be

  "The United States of America".

II.

Each state retains its sovereignty, freedom, and independence, and every power, jurisdiction, and right, which is not by this Confederation expressly delegated to the United States, in Congress assembled.

III.

The said States hereby severally enter into a firm league of friendship with each other, for their common defense, the security of their liberties, and their mutual and general welfare, binding themselves to assist each other, against all force offered to, or attacks made upon them, or any of them, on account of religion, sovereignty, trade, or any other pretense whatever.

IV.

The better to secure and perpetuate mutual friendship and intercourse among the people of the different States in this Union, the free inhabitants of each of these States, paupers, vagabonds, and fugitives from justice excepted, shall be entitled to all privileges and immunities of free citizens in the several States; and the people of each State shall free ingress and regress to and from any other State, and shall enjoy therein all the privileges of trade and commerce, subject to the same duties, impositions, and restrictions as the inhabitants thereof respectively, provided that such restrictions shall not extend so far as to prevent the removal of property imported into any State, to any other State, of which the owner is an inhabitant; provided also that no imposition, duties or restriction shall be laid by any State, on the property of the United States, or either of them.

If any person guilty of, or charged with, treason, felony, or other high misdemeanor in any State, shall flee from justice, and be found in any of the United States, he shall, upon demand of the Governor or executive power of the State from which he fled, be delivered up and removed to the State having jurisdiction of his offense.

Full faith and credit shall be given in each of these States to the records, acts, and judicial proceedings of the courts and magistrates of every other State.

V.

For the most convenient management of the general interests of the United States, delegates shall be annually appointed in such manner as the legislatures of each State shall direct, to meet in Congress on the first Monday in November, in every year, with a powerreserved to each State to recall its delegates, or any of them, at any time within the year, and to send others in their stead for the remainder of the year.

No State shall be represented in Congress by less than two, nor more than seven members; and no person shall be capable of being a delegate for more than three years in any term of six years; nor shall any person, being a delegate, be capable of holding any office under the United States, for which he, or another for his benefit, receives any salary, fees or emolument of any kind.

Each State shall maintain its own delegates in a meeting of the States, and while they act as members of the committee of the States.

In determining questions in the United States in Congress assembled, each State shall have one vote.

Freedom of speech and debate in Congress shall not be impeached or questioned in any court or place out of Congress, and the members of Congress shall be protected in their persons from arrests or imprisonments, during the time of their going to and from, and attendence on Congress, except for treason, felony, or breach of the peace.

VI.

No State, without the consent of the United States in Congress assembled, shall send any embassy to, or receive any embassy from, or enter into any conference, agreement, alliance or treaty with any King, Prince or State; nor shall any person holding any office of profit or trust under the United States, or any of them, accept any present, emolument, office or title of any kind whatever from any King, Prince or foreign State; nor shall the United States in Congress assembled, or any of them, grant any title of nobility.

No two or more States shall enter into any treaty, confederation or alliance whatever between them, without the consent of the United States in Congress assembled, specifying accurately the purposes for which the same is to be entered into, and how long it shall continue.

No State shall lay any imposts or duties, which may interfere with any stipulations in treaties, entered into by the United States in Congress assembled, with any King, Prince or State, in pursuance of any treaties already proposed by Congress, to the courts of France and Spain.

No vessel of war shall be kept up in time of peace by any State, except such number only, as shall be deemed necessary by the United States in Congress assembled, for the defense of such State, or its trade; nor shall any body of forces be kept up by any State in time of peace, except such number only, as in the judgement of the United States in Congress assembled, shall be deemed requisite to garrison the forts necessary for the defense of such State; but every State shall always keep up a well-regulated and disciplined militia, sufficiently armed and accoutered, and shall provide and constantly have ready for use, in public stores, a due number of filed pieces and tents, and a proper quantity of arms, ammunition and camp equipage.

No State shall engage in any war without the consent of the United States in Congress assembled, unless such State be actually invaded by enemies, or shall have received certain advice of a resolution being formed by some nation of Indians to invade such State, and the danger is so imminent as not to admit of a delay till the United States in Congress assembled can be consulted; nor shall any State grant commissions to any ships or vessels of war, nor letters of marque or reprisal, except it be after a declaration of war by the United States in Congress assembled, and then only against the Kingdom or State and the subjects thereof, against which war has been so declared, and under such regulations as shall be established by the United States in Congress assembled, unless such State be infested by pirates, in which case vessels of war may be fitted out for that occasion, and kept so long as the danger shall continue, or until the United States in Congress assembled shall determine otherwise.

VII.

When land forces are raised by any State for the common defense, all officers of or under the rank of colonel, shall be appointed by the legislature of each State respectively, by whom such forces shall be raised, or in such manner as such State shall direct, and all vacancies shall be filled up by the State which first made the appointment.

VIII.

All charges of war, and all other expenses that shall be incurred for the common defense or general welfare, and allowed by the United States in Congress assembled, shall be defrayed out of a common treasury, which shall be supplied by the several States in proportion to the value of all land within each State, granted or surveyed for any person, as such land and the buildings and improvements thereon shall be estimated according to such mode as the United States in Congress assembled, shall from time to time direct and appoint.

The taxes for paying that proportion shall be laid and levied by the authority and direction of the legislatures of the several States within the time agreed upon by the United States in Congress assembled.

IX.

The United States in Congress assembled, shall have the sole and exclusive right and power of determining on peace and war, except in the cases mentioned in the sixth article -- of sending and receiving ambassadors -- entering into treaties and alliances, provided that no treaty of commerce shall be made whereby the legislative power of the respective States shall be restrained from imposing such imposts and duties on foreigners, as their own people are subjected to, or from prohibiting the exportation or importation of any species of goods or commodities whatsoever -- of establishing rules for deciding in all cases, what captures on land or water shall be legal, and in what manner prizes taken by land or naval forces in the service of the United States shall be divided or appropriated -- of granting letters of marque and reprisal in times of peace -- appointing courts for the trial of piracies and felonies commited on the high seas and establishing courts for receiving and determining finally appeals in all cases of captures, provided that no member of Congress shall be appointed a judge of any of the said courts.

The United States in Congress assembled shall also be the last resort on appeal in all disputes and differences now subsisting or that hereafter may arise between two or more States concerning boundary, jurisdiction or any other causes whatever; which authority shall always be exercised in the manner following. Whenever the legislative or executive authority or lawful agent of any State in controversy with another shall present a petition to Congress stating the matter in question and praying for a hearing, notice thereof shall be given by order of Congress to the legislative or executive authority of the other State in controversy, and a day assigned for the appearance of the parties by their lawful agents, who shall then be directed to appoint by joint consent, commissioners or judges to constitute a court for hearing and determining the matter in question: but if they cannot agree, Congress shall name three persons out of each of the United States, and from the list of such persons each party shall alternately strike out one, the petitioners beginning, until the number shall be reduced to thirteen; and from that number not less than seven, nor more than nine names as Congress shall direct, shall in the presence of Congress be drawn out by lot, and the persons whose names shall be so drawn or any five of them, shall be commissioners or judges, to hear and finally determine the controversy, so always as a major part of the judges who shall hear the cause shall agree in the determination: and if either party shall neglect to attend at the day appointed, without showing reasons, which Congress shall judge sufficient, or being present shall refuse to strike, the Congress shall proceed to nominate three persons out of each State, and the secretary of Congress shall strike in behalf of such party absent or refusing; and the judgement and sentence of the court to be appointed, in the manner before prescribed, shall be final and conclusive; and if any of the parties shall refuse to submit to the authority of such court, or to appear or defend their claim or cause, the court shall nevertheless proceed to pronounce sentence, or judgement, which shall in like manner be final and decisive, the judgement or sentence and other proceedings being in either case transmitted to Congress, and lodged among the acts of Congress for the security of the parties concerned: provided that every commissioner, before he sits in judgement, shall take an oath to be administered by one of the judges of the supreme or superior court of the State, where the cause shall be tried, 'well and truly to hear and determine the matter in question, according to the best of his judgement, without favor, affection or hope of reward': provided also, that no State shall be deprived of territory for the benefit of the United States.

All controversies concerning the private right of soil claimed under different grants of two or more States, whose jurisdictions as they may respect such lands, and the States which passed such grants are adjusted, the said grants or either of them being at the same time claimed to have originated antecedent to such settlement of jurisdiction, shall on the petition of either party to the Congress of the United States, be finally determined as near as may be in the same manner as is before presecribed for deciding disputes respecting territorial jurisdiction between different States.

The United States in Congress assembled shall also have the sole and exclusive right and power of regulating the alloy and value of coin struck by their own authority, or by that of the respective States -- fixing the standards of weights and measures throughout the United States -- regulating the trade and managing all affairs with the Indians, not members of any of the States, provided that the legislative right of any State within its own limits be not infringed or violated -- establishing or regulating post offices from one State to another, throughout all the United States, and exacting such postage on the papers passing through the same as may be requisite to defray the expenses of the said office -- appointing all officers of the land forces, in the service of the United States, excepting regimental officers -- appointing all the officers of the naval forces, and commissioning all officers whatever in the service of the United States -- making rules for the government and regulation of the said land and naval forces, and directing their operations.

The United States in Congress assembled shall have authority to appoint a committee, to sit in the recess of Congress, to be denominated 'A Committee of the States', and to consist of one delegate from each State; and to appoint such other committees and civil officers as may be necessary for managing the general affairs of the United States under their direction -- to appoint one of their members to preside, provided that no person be allowed to serve in the office of president more than one year in any term of three years; to ascertain the necessary sums of money to be raised for the service of the United States, and to appropriate and apply the same for defraying the public expenses -- to borrow money, or emit bills on the credit of the United States, transmitting every half-year to the respective States an account of the sums of money so borrowed or emitted -- to build and equip a navy -- to agree upon the number of land forces, and to make requisitions from each State for its quota, in proportion to the number of white inhabitants in such State; which requisition shall be binding, and thereupon the legislature of each State shall appoint the regimental officers, raise the men and cloath, arm and equip them in a solid-like manner, at the expense of the United States; and the officers and men so cloathed, armed and equipped shall march to the place appointed, and within the time agreed on by the United States in Congress assembled. But if the United States in Congress assembled shall, on consideration of circumstances judge proper that any State should not raise men, or should raise a smaller number of men than the quota thereof, such extra number shall be raised, officered, cloathed, armed and equipped in the same manner as the quota of each State, unless the legislature of such State shall judge that such extra number cannot be safely spread out in the same, in which case they shall raise, officer, cloath, arm and equip as many of such extra number as they judeg can be safely spared. And the officers and men so cloathed, armed, and equipped, shall march to the place appointed, and within the time agreed on by the United States in Congress assembled.

The United States in Congress assembled shall never engage in a war, nor grant letters of marque or reprisal in time of peace, nor enter into any treaties or alliances, nor coin money, nor regulate the value thereof, nor ascertain the sums and expenses necessary for the defense and welfare of the United States, or any of them, nor emit bills, nor borrow money on the credit of the United States, nor appropriate money, nor agree upon the number of vessels of war, to be built or purchased, or the number of land or sea forces to be raised, nor appoint a commander in chief of the army or navy, unless nine States assent to the same: nor shall a question on any other point, except for adjourning from day to day be determined, unless by the votes of the majority of the United States in Congress assembled.

The Congress of the United States shall have power to adjourn to any time within the year, and to any place within the United States, so that no period of adjournment be for a longer duration than the space of six months, and shall publish the journal of their proceedings monthly, except such parts thereof relating to treaties, alliances or military operations, as in their judgement require secrecy; and the yeas and nays of the delegates of each State on any question shall be entered on the journal, when it is desired by any delegates of a State, or any of them, at his or their request shall be furnished with a transcript of the said journal, except such parts as are above excepted, to lay before the legislatures of the several States.

X.

The Committee of the States, or any nine of them, shall be authorized to execute, in the recess of Congress, such of the powers of Congress as the United States in Congress assembled, by the consent of the nine States, shall from time to time think expedient to vest them with; provided that no power be delegated to the said

Committee, for the exercise of which, by the Articles of Confederation, the voice of nine States in the Congress of the United States assembled be requisite.

XI.

Canada acceding to this confederation, and adjoining in the measures of the United States, shall be admitted into, and entitled to all the advantages of this Union; but no other colony shall be admitted into the same, unless such admission be agreed to by nine States.

XII.

All bills of credit emitted, monies borrowed, and debts contracted by, or under the authority of Congress, before the assembling of the United States, in pursuance of the present confederation, shall be deemed and considered as a charge against the United States, for payment and satisfaction whereof the said United States, and the public faith are hereby solemnly pleged.

XIII.

Every State shall abide by the determination of the United States in Congress assembled, on all questions which by this confederation are submitted to them. And the Articles of this Confederation shall be inviolably observed by every State, and the Union shall be perpetual; nor shall any alteration at any time hereafter be made in any of them; unless such alteration be agreed to in a Congress of the United States, and be afterwards confirmed by the legislatures of every State.

And Whereas it hath pleased the Great Governor of the World to incline the hearts of the legislatures we respectively represent in Congress, to approve of, and to authorize us to ratify the said Articles of Confederation and perpetual Union. Know Ye that we the undersigned delegates, by virtue of the power and authority to us given for that purpose, do by these presents, in the name and in behalf of our respective constituents, fully and entirely ratify and confirm each and every of the said Articles of Confederation and perpetual Union, and all and singular the matters and things therein contained: And we do further solemnly plight and engage the faith of our respective constituents, that they shall abide by the determinations of the United States in Congress assembled, on all questions, which by the said Confederation are submitted to them. And that the Articles thereof shall be inviolably observed by the States we respectively represent, and that the Union shall be perpetual.

In Witness whereof we have hereunto set our hands in Congress. Done at Philadelphia in the State of Pennsylvania the ninth day of July in the Year of our Lord One Thousand Seven Hundred and Seventy-Eight, and in the Third Year of the independence of America.

Agreed to by Congress 15 November 1777 In force after ratification by Maryland, 1 March 1781

Appendix B: The Constitution of the United States of America (un-annotated)

We the People of the United States, in Order to form a more perfect Union, establish Justice, insure domestic Tranquility, provide for the common defence, promote the general Welfare, and secure the Blessings of Liberty to ourselves and our Posterity, do ordain and establish this Constitution for the United States of America.

Article. I.

Section. 1.

All legislative Powers herein granted shall be vested in a Congress of the United States, which shall consist of a Senate and House of Representatives.

Section. 2.

The House of Representatives shall be composed of Members chosen every second Year by the People of the several States, and the Electors in each State shall have the Qualifications requisite for Electors of the most numerous Branch of the State Legislature.

No Person shall be a Representative who shall not have attained to the Age of twenty five Years, and been seven Years a Citizen of the United States, and who shall not, when elected, be an Inhabitant of that State in which he shall be chosen.

Representatives and direct Taxes shall be apportioned among the several States which may be included within this Union, according to their respective Numbers, which shall be determined by adding to the whole Number of free Persons, including those bound to Service for a Term of Years, and excluding Indians not taxed, three fifths of all other Persons. The actual Enumeration shall be made within three Years after the first Meeting of the Congress of the United States, and within every subsequent Term of ten Years, in such Manner as they shall by Law direct. The Number of Representatives shall not exceed one for every thirty Thousand, but each State shall have at Least one Representative; and until such enumeration shall be made, the State of New Hampshire shall be entitled to chuse three, Massachusetts eight, Rhode-Island and Providence Plantations one, Connecticut five, New-York six, New Jersey four, Pennsylvania eight, Delaware one, Maryland six, Virginia ten, North Carolina five, South Carolina five, and Georgia three.

When vacancies happen in the Representation from any State, the Executive Authority thereof shall issue Writs of Election to fill such Vacancies.

The House of Representatives shall chuse their Speaker and other Officers; and shall have the sole Power of Impeachment.

Section. 3.

The Senate of the United States shall be composed of two Senators from each State, chosen by the Legislature thereof, for six Years; and each Senator shall have one Vote.

Immediately after they shall be assembled in Consequence of the first Election, they shall be divided as equally as may be into three Classes. The Seats of the Senators of the first Class shall be vacated at the Expiration of the second Year, of the second Class at the Expiration of the fourth Year, and of the third Class at the Expiration of the sixth Year, so that one third may be chosen every second Year; and if Vacancies happen by Resignation, or otherwise, during the Recess of the Legislature of any State, the Executive thereof may make temporary Appointments until the next Meeting of the Legislature, which shall then fill such Vacancies.

No Person shall be a Senator who shall not have attained to the Age of thirty Years, and been nine Years a Citizen of the United States, and who shall not, when elected, be an Inhabitant of that State for which he shall be chosen.

The Vice President of the United States shall be President of the Senate, but shall have no Vote, unless they be equally divided.

The Senate shall chuse their other Officers, and also a President pro tempore, in the Absence of the Vice President, or when he shall exercise the Office of President of the United States.

The Senate shall have the sole Power to try all Impeachments. When sitting for that Purpose, they shall be on Oath or Affirmation. When the President of the United States is tried, the Chief Justice shall preside: And no Person shall be convicted without the Concurrence of two thirds of the Members present.

Judgment in Cases of Impeachment shall not extend further than to removal from Office, and disqualification to hold and enjoy any Office of honor, Trust or Profit under the United States: but the Party convicted shall nevertheless be liable and subject to Indictment, Trial, Judgment and Punishment, according to Law.

Section. 4.

The Times, Places and Manner of holding Elections for Senators and Representatives, shall be prescribed in each State by the Legislature thereof; but the Congress may at any time by Law make or alter such Regulations, except as to the Places of chusing Senators.

The Congress shall assemble at least once in every Year, and such Meeting shall be on the first Monday in December, unless they shall by Law appoint a different Day.

Section. 5.

Each House shall be the Judge of the Elections, Returns and Qualifications of its own Members, and a Majority of each shall constitute a Quorum to do Business; but a smaller Number may adjourn from day to day, and may be authorized to compel the Attendance of absent Members, in such Manner, and under such Penalties as each House may provide.

Each House may determine the Rules of its Proceedings, punish its Members for disorderly Behaviour, and, with the Concurrence of two thirds, expel a Member.

Each House shall keep a Journal of its Proceedings, and from time to time publish the same, excepting such Parts as may in their Judgment require Secrecy; and the Yeas and Nays of the Members of either House on any question shall, at the Desire of one fifth of those Present, be entered on the Journal.

Neither House, during the Session of Congress, shall, without the Consent of the other, adjourn for more than three days, nor to any other Place than that in which the two Houses shall be sitting.

Section. 6.

The Senators and Representatives shall receive a Compensation for their Services, to be ascertained by Law, and paid out of the Treasury of the United States. They shall in all Cases, except Treason, Felony and Breach of the Peace, be privileged from Arrest during their Attendance at the Session of their respective Houses, and in going to and returning from the same; and for any Speech or Debate in either House, they shall not be questioned in any other Place.

No Senator or Representative shall, during the Time for which he was elected, be appointed to any civil Office under the Authority of the United States, which shall have been created, or the Emoluments whereof shall have been encreased during such time; and no Person holding any Office under the United States, shall be a Member of either House during his Continuance in Office.

Section. 7.

All Bills for raising Revenue shall originate in the House of Representatives; but the Senate may propose or concur with Amendments as on other Bills.

Every Bill which shall have passed the House of Representatives and the Senate, shall, before it become a Law, be presented to the President of the United States; If he approve he shall sign it, but if not he shall return it, with his Objections to that House in which it shall have originated, who shall enter the Objections at large on their Journal, and proceed to reconsider it. If after such Reconsideration two thirds of that House shall agree to pass the Bill, it shall be sent, together with the Objections, to the other House, by which it shall likewise be reconsidered, and if approved by two thirds of that House, it shall become a Law. But in all such Cases the Votes of both Houses shall be determined by yeas and Nays, and the Names of the Persons voting for and against the Bill shall be entered on the Journal of each House respectively. If any Bill shall not be returned by the President within ten Days (Sundays excepted) after it shall have been presented to him, the Same shall be a Law, in like Manner as if he had signed it, unless the Congress by their Adjournment prevent its Return, in which Case it shall not be a Law.

Every Order, Resolution, or Vote to which the Concurrence of the Senate and House of Representatives may be necessary (except on a question of Adjournment) shall be presented to the President of the United States; and before the Same shall take Effect, shall be approved by him, or being disapproved by him, shall be repassed by two thirds of the Senate and House of Representatives, according to the Rules and Limitations prescribed in the Case of a Bill.

Section. 8.

The Congress shall have Power To lay and collect Taxes, Duties, Imposts and Excises, to pay the Debts and provide for the common Defence and general

Welfare of the United States; but all Duties, Imposts and Excises shall be uniform throughout the United States;

To borrow Money on the credit of the United States;

To regulate Commerce with foreign Nations, and among the several States, and with the Indian Tribes;

To establish an uniform Rule of Naturalization, and uniform Laws on the subject of Bankruptcies throughout the United States;

To coin Money, regulate the Value thereof, and of foreign Coin, and fix the Standard of Weights and Measures;

To provide for the Punishment of counterfeiting the Securities and current Coin of the United States;

To establish Post Offices and post Roads;

To promote the Progress of Science and useful Arts, by securing for limited Times to Authors and Inventors the exclusive Right to their respective Writings and Discoveries;

To constitute Tribunals inferior to the supreme Court;

To define and punish Piracies and Felonies committed on the high Seas, and Offences against the Law of Nations;

To declare War, grant Letters of Marque and Reprisal, and make Rules concerning Captures on Land and Water;

To raise and support Armies, but no Appropriation of Money to that Use shall be for a longer Term than two Years;

To provide and maintain a Navy;

To make Rules for the Government and Regulation of the land and naval Forces;

To provide for calling forth the Militia to execute the Laws of the Union, suppress Insurrections and repel Invasions;

To provide for organizing, arming, and disciplining, the Militia, and for governing such Part of them as may be employed in the Service of the United States, reserving to the States respectively, the Appointment of the Officers, and the Authority of training the Militia according to the discipline prescribed by Congress;

To exercise exclusive Legislation in all Cases whatsoever, over such District (not exceeding ten Miles square) as may, by Cession of particular States, and the Acceptance of Congress, become the Seat of the Government of the United States, and to exercise like Authority over all Places purchased by the Consent of the Legislature of the State in which the Same shall be, for the Erection of Forts, Magazines, Arsenals, dock-Yards, and other needful Buildings;—And

To make all Laws which shall be necessary and proper for carrying into Execution the foregoing Powers, and all other Powers vested by this Constitution in the Government of the United States, or in any Department or Officer thereof.

Section. 9.

The Migration or Importation of such Persons as any of the States now existing shall think proper to admit, shall not be prohibited by the Congress prior to the Year one thousand eight hundred and eight, but a Tax or duty may be imposed on such Importation, not exceeding ten dollars for each Person.

The Privilege of the Writ of Habeas Corpus shall not be suspended, unless when in Cases of Rebellion or Invasion the public Safety may require it.

No Bill of Attainder or ex post facto Law shall be passed.

No Capitation, or other direct, Tax shall be laid, unless in Proportion to the Census or enumeration herein before directed to be taken.

No Tax or Duty shall be laid on Articles exported from any State.

No Preference shall be given by any Regulation of Commerce or Revenue to the Ports of one State over those of another: nor shall Vessels bound to, or from, one State, be obliged to enter, clear, or pay Duties in another.

No Money shall be drawn from the Treasury, but in Consequence of Appropriations made by Law; and a regular Statement and Account of the Receipts and Expenditures of all public Money shall be published from time to time.

No Title of Nobility shall be granted by the United States: And no Person holding any Office of Profit or Trust under them, shall, without the Consent of the Congress, accept of any present, Emolument, Office, or Title, of any kind whatever, from any King, Prince, or foreign State.

Section. 10.

No State shall enter into any Treaty, Alliance, or Confederation; grant Letters of Marque and Reprisal; coin Money; emit Bills of Credit; make any Thing but gold and silver Coin a Tender in Payment of Debts; pass any Bill of Attainder, ex post facto Law, or Law impairing the Obligation of Contracts, or grant any Title of Nobility.

No State shall, without the Consent of the Congress, lay any Imposts or Duties on Imports or Exports, except what may be absolutely necessary for executing it's inspection Laws: and the net Produce of all Duties and Imposts, laid by any State on Imports or Exports, shall be for the Use of the Treasury of the United States; and all such Laws shall be subject to the Revision and Controul of the Congress.

No State shall, without the Consent of Congress, lay any Duty of Tonnage, keep Troops, or Ships of War in time of Peace, enter into any Agreement or Compact with another State, or with a foreign Power, or engage in War, unless actually invaded, or in such imminent Danger as will not admit of delay.

Article. II.

Section. 1.

The executive Power shall be vested in a President of the United States of America. He shall hold his Office during the Term of four Years, and, together with the Vice President, chosen for the same Term, be elected, as follows

Each State shall appoint, in such Manner as the Legislature thereof may direct, a Number of Electors, equal to the whole Number of Senators and Representatives to which the State may be entitled in the Congress: but no Senator or Representative, or Person holding an Office of Trust or Profit under the United States, shall be appointed an Elector.

The Electors shall meet in their respective States, and vote by Ballot for two Persons, of whom one at least shall not be an Inhabitant of the same State with themselves. And they shall make a List of all the Persons voted for, and of the Number of Votes for each; which List they shall sign and certify, and transmit sealed to the Seat of the Government of the United States, directed to the President of the Senate. The President of the Senate shall, in the Presence of the Senate and House of Representatives, open all the Certificates, and the Votes shall then be counted. The Person having the greatest Number of Votes shall be the President, if such Number be a Majority of the whole Number of Electors appointed; and if there be more than one who have such Majority, and have an equal Number of Votes, then the House of Representatives shall immediately chuse by Ballot one of them for President; and if no Person have a Majority, then from the five highest on the List the said House shall in like Manner chuse the President. But in chusing the President, the Votes shall be taken by States, the Representation from each State having one Vote; A quorum for this Purpose shall consist of a Member or Members from two thirds of the States, and a Majority of all the States shall be necessary to a Choice. In every Case, after the Choice of the President, the Person having the greatest Number of Votes of the Electors shall be the Vice President. But if there should remain two or more who have equal Votes, the Senate shall chuse from them by Ballot the Vice President.

The Congress may determine the Time of chusing the Electors, and the Day on which they shall give their Votes; which Day shall be the same throughout the United States.

No Person except a natural born Citizen, or a Citizen of the United States, at the time of the Adoption of this Constitution, shall be eligible to the Office of President; neither shall any Person be eligible to that Office who shall not have attained to the Age of thirty five Years, and been fourteen Years a Resident within the United States.

In Case of the Removal of the President from Office, or of his Death, Resignation, or Inability to discharge the Powers and Duties of the said Office, the Same shall devolve on the Vice President, and the Congress may by Law provide for the Case of Removal, Death, Resignation or Inability, both of the President and Vice President, declaring what Officer shall then act as President, and such Officer shall act accordingly, until the Disability be removed, or a President shall be elected.

188

The President shall, at stated Times, receive for his Services, a Compensation, which shall neither be encreased nor diminished during the Period for which he shall have been elected, and he shall not receive within that Period any other Emolument from the United States, or any of them.

Before he enter on the Execution of his Office, he shall take the following Oath or Affirmation:—"I do solemnly swear (or affirm) that I will faithfully execute the Office of President of the United States, and will to the best of my Ability, preserve, protect and defend the Constitution of the United States."

Section. 2.

The President shall be Commander in Chief of the Army and Navy of the United States, and of the Militia of the several States, when called into the actual Service of the United States; he may require the Opinion, in writing, of the principal Officer in each of the executive Departments, upon any Subject relating to the Duties of their respective Offices, and he shall have Power to grant Reprieves and Pardons for Offences against the United States, except in Cases of Impeachment.

He shall have Power, by and with the Advice and Consent of the Senate, to make Treaties, provided two thirds of the Senators present concur; and he shall nominate, and by and with the Advice and Consent of the Senate, shall appoint Ambassadors, other public Ministers and Consuls, Judges of the supreme Court, and all other Officers of the United States, whose Appointments are not herein otherwise provided for, and which shall be established by Law: but the Congress may by Law vest the Appointment of such inferior Officers, as they think proper, in the President alone, in the Courts of Law, or in the Heads of Departments.

The President shall have Power to fill up all Vacancies that may happen during the Recess of the Senate, by granting Commissions which shall expire at the End of their next Session.

Section. 3.

He shall from time to time give to the Congress Information of the State of the Union, and recommend to their Consideration such Measures as he shall judge necessary and expedient; he may, on extraordinary Occasions, convene both Houses, or either of them, and in Case of Disagreement between them, with Respect to the Time of Adjournment, he may adjourn them to such Time as he shall think proper; he shall receive Ambassadors and other public Ministers; he shall take Care that the Laws be faithfully executed, and shall Commission all the Officers of the United States.

Section. 4.

The President, Vice President and all civil Officers of the United States, shall be removed from Office on Impeachment for, and Conviction of, Treason, Bribery, or other high Crimes and Misdemeanors.

Article III.

Section. 1.

The judicial Power of the United States, shall be vested in one supreme Court, and in such inferior Courts as the Congress may from time to time ordain and establish. The Judges, both of the supreme and inferior Courts, shall hold their Offices during good Behaviour, and shall, at stated Times, receive for their Services, a Compensation, which shall not be diminished during their Continuance in Office.

Section. 2.

The judicial Power shall extend to all Cases, in Law and Equity, arising under this Constitution, the Laws of the United States, and Treaties made, or which shall be made, under their Authority;—to all Cases affecting Ambassadors, other public Ministers and Consuls;—to all Cases of admiralty and maritime Jurisdiction;—to Controversies to which the United States shall be a Party;—to Controversies between two or more States;— between a State and Citizens of another State,— between Citizens of different States,—between Citizens of the same State claiming Lands under Grants of different States, and between a State, or the Citizens thereof, and foreign States, Citizens or Subjects.

In all Cases affecting Ambassadors, other public Ministers and Consuls, and those in which a State shall be Party, the supreme Court shall have original Jurisdiction. In all the other Cases before mentioned, the supreme Court shall have appellate Jurisdiction, both as to Law and Fact, with such Exceptions, and under such Regulations as the Congress shall make.

The Trial of all Crimes, except in Cases of Impeachment, shall be by Jury; and such Trial shall be held in the State where the said Crimes shall have been committed; but when not committed within any State, the Trial shall be at such Place or Places as the Congress may by Law have directed.

Section. 3.

Treason against the United States, shall consist only in levying War against them, or in adhering to their Enemies, giving them Aid and Comfort. No Person shall be convicted of Treason unless on the Testimony of two Witnesses to the same overt Act, or on Confession in open Court.

The Congress shall have Power to declare the Punishment of Treason, but no Attainder of Treason shall work Corruption of Blood, or Forfeiture except during the Life of the Person attainted.

Article. IV.

Section. 1.

Full Faith and Credit shall be given in each State to the public Acts, Records, and judicial Proceedings of every other State. And the Congress may by general Laws prescribe the Manner in which such Acts, Records and Proceedings shall be proved, and the Effect thereof.

Section. 2.

The Citizens of each State shall be entitled to all Privileges and Immunities of Citizens in the several States.

A Person charged in any State with Treason, Felony, or other Crime, who shall flee from Justice, and be found in another State, shall on Demand of the executive Authority of the State from which he fled, be delivered up, to be removed to the State having Jurisdiction of the Crime.

No Person held to Service or Labour in one State, under the Laws thereof, escaping into another, shall, in Consequence of any Law or Regulation therein, be discharged from such Service or Labour, but shall be delivered up on Claim of the Party to whom such Service or Labour may be due.
Section. 3.

New States may be admitted by the Congress into this Union; but no new State shall be formed or erected within the Jurisdiction of any other State; nor any State be formed by the Junction of two or more States, or Parts of States, without the Consent of the Legislatures of the States concerned as well as of the Congress.

The Congress shall have Power to dispose of and make all needful Rules and Regulations respecting the Territory or other Property belonging to the United States; and nothing in this Constitution shall be so construed as to Prejudice any Claims of the United States, or of any particular State.

Section. 4.

The United States shall guarantee to every State in this Union a Republican Form of Government, and shall protect each of them against Invasion; and on Application of the Legislature, or of the Executive (when the Legislature cannot be convened), against domestic Violence.

Article. V.

The Congress, whenever two thirds of both Houses shall deem it necessary, shall propose Amendments to this Constitution, or, on the Application of the Legislatures of two thirds of the several States, shall call a Convention for proposing Amendments, which, in either Case, shall be valid to all Intents and Purposes, as Part of this Constitution, when ratified by the Legislatures of three fourths of the several States, or by Conventions in three fourths thereof, as the one or the other Mode of Ratification may be proposed by the Congress; Provided that no Amendment which may be made prior to the Year One thousand eight hundred and eight shall in any Manner affect the first and fourth Clauses in the Ninth Section of the first Article; and that no State, without its Consent, shall be deprived of its equal Suffrage in the Senate.

Article. VI.

All Debts contracted and Engagements entered into, before the Adoption of this Constitution, shall be as valid against the United States under this Constitution, as under the Confederation.

This Constitution, and the Laws of the United States which shall be made in Pursuance thereof; and all Treaties made, or which shall be made, under the Authority of the United States, shall be the supreme Law of the Land; and the

Judges in every State shall be bound thereby, any Thing in the Constitution or Laws of any State to the Contrary notwithstanding.

The Senators and Representatives before mentioned, and the Members of the several State Legislatures, and all executive and judicial Officers, both of the United States and of the several States, shall be bound by Oath or Affirmation, to support this Constitution; but no religious Test shall ever be required as a Qualification to any Office or public Trust under the United States.

Article. VII.

The Ratification of the Conventions of nine States, shall be sufficient for the Establishment of this Constitution between the States so ratifying the Same.

The Word, "the," being interlined between the seventh and eighth Lines of the first Page, The Word "Thirty" being partly written on an Erazure in the fifteenth Line of the first Page, The Words "is tried" being interlined between the thirty second and thirty third Lines of the first Page and the Word "the" being interlined between the forty third and forty fourth Lines of the second Page.

Attest William Jackson Secretary

done in Convention by the Unanimous Consent of the States present the Seventeenth Day of September in the Year of our Lord one thousand seven hundred and Eighty seven and of the Independance of the United States of America the Twelfth In witness whereof We have hereunto subscribed our Names,

G°. Washington
Presidt and deputy from Virginia
Delaware

Geo: Read
Gunning Bedford jun
John Dickinson
Richard Bassett
Jaco: Broom
Maryland

James McHenry
Dan of St Thos. Jenifer

Danl. Carroll
Virginia

John Blair
James Madison Jr.
North Carolina

Wm. Blount
Richd. Dobbs Spaight
Hu Williamson
South Carolina

J. Rutledge
Charles Cotesworth Pinckney
Charles Pinckney
Pierce Butler
Georgia

William Few
Abr Baldwin
New Hampshire

John Langdon
Nicholas Gilman
Massachusetts

Nathaniel Gorham
Rufus King
Connecticut

Wm. Saml. Johnson
Roger Sherman
New York

Alexander Hamilton
New Jersey

Wil: Livingston
David Brearley
Wm. Paterson

Jona: Dayton
Pennsylvania

B Franklin
Thomas Mifflin
Robt. Morris
Geo. Clymer
Thos. FitzSimons
Jared Ingersoll
James Wilson
Gouv Morris

Amendment I

Congress shall make no law respecting an establishment of religion, or prohibiting the free exercise thereof; or abridging the freedom of speech, or of the press; or the right of the people peaceably to assemble, and to petition the Government for a redress of grievances.

Amendment II

A well regulated Militia, being necessary to the security of a free State, the right of the people to keep and bear Arms, shall not be infringed.

Amendment III

No Soldier shall, in time of peace be quartered in any house, without the consent of the Owner, nor in time of war, but in a manner to be prescribed by law.

Amendment IV

The right of the people to be secure in their persons, houses, papers, and effects, against unreasonable searches and seizures, shall not be violated, and no Warrants shall issue, but upon probable cause, supported by Oath or affirmation, and particularly describing the place to be searched, and the persons or things to be seized.

Amendment V

No person shall be held to answer for a capital, or otherwise infamous crime, unless on a presentment or indictment of a Grand Jury, except in cases arising in the land or naval forces, or in the Militia, when in actual service in time of War or public danger; nor shall any person be subject for the same offence to be twice put in jeopardy of life or limb; nor shall be compelled in any criminal case to be a witness against himself, nor be deprived of life, liberty, or property, without due process of law; nor shall private property be taken for public use, without just compensation.

Amendment VI

In all criminal prosecutions, the accused shall enjoy the right to a speedy and public trial, by an impartial jury of the State and district wherein the crime shall have been committed, which district shall have been previously ascertained by law, and to be informed of the nature and cause of the accusation; to be confronted with the witnesses against him; to have compulsory process for obtaining witnesses in his favor, and to have the Assistance of Counsel for his defence.

Amendment VII

In Suits at common law, where the value in controversy shall exceed twenty dollars, the right of trial by jury shall be preserved, and no fact tried by a jury, shall be otherwise re-examined in any Court of the United States, than according to the rules of the common law.

Amendment VIII

Excessive bail shall not be required, nor excessive fines imposed, nor cruel and unusual punishments inflicted.

Amendment IX

The enumeration in the Constitution, of certain rights, shall not be construed to deny or disparage others retained by the people.

Amendment X

The powers not delegated to the United States by the Constitution, nor prohibited by it to the States, are reserved to the States respectively, or to the people.

Amendment XI

The Judicial power of the United States shall not be construed to extend to any suit in law or equity, commenced or prosecuted against one of the United States by Citizens of another State, or by Citizens or Subjects of any Foreign State.

Amendment XII

The Electors shall meet in their respective states, and vote by ballot for President and Vice-President, one of whom, at least, shall not be an inhabitant of the same state with themselves; they shall name in their ballots the person voted for as President, and in distinct ballots the person voted for as Vice-President, and they shall make distinct lists of all persons voted for as President, and of all persons voted for as Vice-President, and of the number of votes for each, which lists they shall sign and certify, and transmit sealed to the seat of the government of the United States, directed to the President of the Senate;—The President of the Senate shall, in the presence of the Senate and House of Representatives, open all the certificates and the votes shall then be counted;—The person having the greatest number of votes for President, shall be the President, if such number be a majority of the whole number of Electors appointed; and if no person have such majority, then from the persons having the highest numbers not exceeding three on the list of those voted for as President, the House of Representatives shall choose immediately, by ballot, the President. But in choosing the President, the votes shall be taken by states, the representation from each state having one vote; a quorum for this purpose shall consist of a member or members from two-thirds of the states, and a majority of all the states shall be necessary to a choice. And if the House of Representatives shall not choose a President whenever the right of choice shall devolve upon them, before the fourth day of March next following, then the Vice-President shall act as President, as in the case of the death or other constitutional disability of the President.14 —The person having the greatest number of votes as Vice-President, shall be the Vice-President, if such number be a majority of the whole number of Electors appointed, and if no person have a majority, then from the two highest numbers on the list, the Senate shall choose the Vice-President; a quorum for the purpose shall consist of two-thirds of the whole number of Senators, and a majority of the whole number shall be necessary to a choice. But no person constitutionally ineligible to the office of President shall be eligible to that of Vice-President of the United States.

Amendment XIII

Neither slavery nor involuntary servitude, except as a punishment for crime whereof the party shall have been duly convicted, shall exist within the United States, or any place subject to their jurisdiction.

Congress shall have power to enforce this article by appropriate legislation.

Amendment XIV

1: All persons born or naturalized in the United States, and subject to the jurisdiction thereof, are citizens of the United States and of the State wherein they reside. No State shall make or enforce any law which shall abridge the privileges or immunities of citizens of the United States; nor shall any State deprive any person of life, liberty, or property, without due process of law; nor deny to any person within its jurisdiction the equal protection of the laws.

2: Representatives shall be apportioned among the several States according to their respective numbers, counting the whole number of persons in each State, excluding Indians not taxed. But when the right to vote at any election for the choice of electors for President and Vice President of the United States, Representatives in Congress, the Executive and Judicial officers of a State, or the members of the Legislature thereof, is denied to any of the male inhabitants of such State, being twenty-one years of age, and citizens of the United States, or in any way abridged, except for participation in rebellion, or other crime, the basis of representation therein shall be reduced in the proportion which the number of such male citizens shall bear to the whole number of male citizens twenty-one years of age in such State.

3: No person shall be a Senator or Representative in Congress, or elector of President and Vice President, or hold any office, civil or military, under the United States, or under any State, who, having previously taken an oath, as a member of Congress, or as an officer of the United States, or as a member of any State legislature, or as an executive or judicial officer of any State, to support the Constitution of the United States, shall have engaged in insurrection or rebellion against the same, or given aid or comfort to the enemies thereof. But Congress may by a vote of two-thirds of each House, remove such disability.

4: The validity of the public debt of the United States, authorized by law, including debts incurred for payment of pensions and bounties for services in suppressing insurrection or rebellion, shall not be questioned. But neither the United States nor any State shall assume or pay any debt or obligation incurred in aid of insurrection or rebellion against the United States, or any claim for the loss or emancipation of any slave; but all such debts, obligations and claims shall be held illegal and void.

5: The Congress shall have power to enforce, by appropriate legislation, the provisions of this article.

Amendment XV

The right of citizens of the United States to vote shall not be denied or abridged by the United States or by any State on account of race, color, or previous condition of servitude.

The Congress shall have power to enforce this article by appropriate legislation.

Amendment XVI

The Congress shall have power to lay and collect taxes on incomes, from whatever source derived, without apportionment among the several States, and without regard to any census or enumeration.

Amendment XVII

1: The Senate of the United States shall be composed of two Senators from each State, elected by the people thereof, for six years; and each Senator shall have one vote. The electors in each State shall have the qualifications requisite for electors of the most numerous branch of the State legislatures.

2: When vacancies happen in the representation of any State in the Senate, the executive authority of such State shall issue writs of election to fill such vacancies: Provided, That the legislature of any State may empower the executive thereof to make temporary appointments until the people fill the vacancies by election as the legislature may direct.

3: This amendment shall not be so construed as to affect the election or term of any Senator chosen before it becomes valid as part of the Constitution.

Amendment XVIII

1: After one year from the ratification of this article the manufacture, sale, or transportation of intoxicating liquors within, the importation thereof into, or the exportation thereof from the United States and all territory subject to the jurisdiction thereof for beverage purposes is hereby prohibited.

2: The Congress and the several States shall have concurrent power to enforce this article by appropriate legislation.

3: This article shall be inoperative unless it shall have been ratified as an amendment to the Constitution by the legislatures of the several States, as provided in the Constitution, within seven years from the date of the submission hereof to the States by the Congress.

Amendment XIX

The right of citizens of the United States to vote shall not be denied or abridged by the United States or by any State on account of sex.

Congress shall have power to enforce this article by appropriate legislation.

Amendment XX

1: The terms of the President and Vice President shall end at noon on the 20th day of January, and the terms of Senators and Representatives at noon on the 3d day of January, of the years in which such terms would have ended if this article had not been ratified; and the terms of their successors shall then begin.

2: The Congress shall assemble at least once in every year, and such meeting shall begin at noon on the 3d day of January, unless they shall by law appoint a different day.

3: If, at the time fixed for the beginning of the term of the President, the President elect shall have died, the Vice President elect shall become President. If a President shall not have been chosen before the time fixed for the beginning of his term, or if the President elect shall have failed to qualify, then the Vice President elect shall act as President until a President shall have qualified; and the Congress may by law provide for the case wherein neither a President elect nor a Vice President elect shall have qualified, declaring who shall then act as President, or the manner in which one who is to act shall be selected, and such person shall act accordingly until a President or Vice President shall have qualified.

4: The Congress may by law provide for the case of the death of any of the persons from whom the House of Representatives may choose a President whenever the right of choice shall have devolved upon them, and for the case of the death of any of the persons from whom the Senate may choose a Vice President whenever the right of choice shall have devolved upon them.

5: Sections 1 and 2 shall take effect on the 15th day of October following the ratification of this article.

6: This article shall be inoperative unless it shall have been ratified as an amendment to the Constitution by the legislatures of three-fourths of the several States within seven years from the date of its submission.

Amendment XXI

1: The eighteenth article of amendment to the Constitution of the United States is hereby repealed.

2: The transportation or importation into any State, Territory, or possession of the United States for delivery or use therein of intoxicating liquors, in violation of the laws thereof, is hereby prohibited.

3: This article shall be inoperative unless it shall have been ratified as an amendment to the Constitution by conventions in the several States, as provided in the Constitution, within seven years from the date of the submission hereof to the States by the Congress.

Amendment XXII

1: No person shall be elected to the office of the President more than twice, and no person who has held the office of President, or acted as President, for more than two years of a term to which some other person was elected President shall be elected to the office of the President more than once. But this article shall not apply to any person holding the office of President when this article was proposed by the Congress, and shall not prevent any person who may be holding the office of President, or acting as President, during the term within which this article becomes operative from holding the office of President or acting as President during the remainder of such term.

2: This article shall be inoperative unless it shall have been ratified as an amendment to the Constitution by the legislatures of three-fourths of the several states within seven years from the date of its submission to the states by the Congress.

Amendment XXIII

1: The District constituting the seat of government of the United States shall appoint in such manner as the Congress may direct: A number of electors of President and Vice President equal to the whole number of Senators and Representatives in Congress to which the District would be entitled if it were a state, but in no event more than the least populous state; they shall be in addition to those appointed by the states, but they shall be considered, for the purposes of the election of President and Vice President, to be electors appointed by a state; and they shall meet in the District and perform such duties as provided by the twelfth article of amendment.

2: The Congress shall have power to enforce this article by appropriate legislation.

Amendment XXIV

1. The right of citizens of the United States to vote in any primary or other election for President or Vice President, for electors for President or Vice President, or for Senator or Representative in Congress, shall not be denied or abridged by the United States or any state by reason of failure to pay any poll tax or other tax.

2. The Congress shall have power to enforce this article by appropriate legislation.

Amendment XXV

1: In case of the removal of the President from office or of his death or resignation, the Vice President shall become President.

2: Whenever there is a vacancy in the office of the Vice President, the President shall nominate a Vice President who shall take office upon confirmation by a majority vote of both Houses of Congress.

3: Whenever the President transmits to the President pro tempore of the Senate and the Speaker of the House of Representatives his written declaration that he is unable to discharge the powers and duties of his office, and until he transmits to them a written declaration to the contrary, such powers and duties shall be discharged by the Vice President as Acting President.

4: Whenever the Vice President and a majority of either the principal officers of the executive departments or of such other body as Congress may by law provide, transmit to the President pro tempore of the Senate and the Speaker of the House of Representatives their written declaration that the President is unable to discharge the powers and duties of his office, the Vice President shall immediately assume the powers and duties of the office as Acting President.

Thereafter, when the President transmits to the President pro tempore of the Senate and the Speaker of the House of Representatives his written declaration that no inability exists, he shall resume the powers and duties of his office unless the Vice President and a majority of either the principal officers of the executive department or of such other body as Congress may by law provide, transmit within four days to the President pro tempore of the Senate and the Speaker of the House of Representatives their written declaration that the President is unable to discharge the powers and duties of his office. Thereupon Congress shall decide the issue, assembling within forty-eight hours for that purpose if not in session. If the Congress, within twenty-one days after receipt of the latter written declaration, or, if Congress is not in session, within twenty-one days after Congress is required to assemble, determines by two-thirds vote of both Houses that the President is unable to discharge the powers and duties of his office, the Vice President shall continue to discharge the same as Acting President; otherwise, the President shall resume the powers and duties of his office.

Amendment XXVI

1: The right of citizens of the United States, who are 18 years of age or older, to vote, shall not be denied or abridged by the United States or any state on account of age.

2: The Congress shall have the power to enforce this article by appropriate legislation.

Amendment XXVII

No law varying the compensation for the services of the Senators and Representatives shall take effect until an election of Representatives shall have intervened.

Appendix C: Provisional Constitution of the Confederate States of America

We, the deputies of the sovereign and independent States of South Carolina, Georgia, Florida, Alabama, Mississippi, and Louisiana, invoking the favor of Almighty God, do hereby, in behalf of these States, ordain and establish this Constitution for the Provisional Government of the same: to continue one year from the inauguration of the President, or until a permanent constitution or confederation between the said States shall be put in operation, whichsoever shall first occur.

ARTICLE I.

Section I. All legislative powers herein delegated shall be vested in this Congress now assembled until otherwise ordained.

Sec. 2. When vacancies happen in the representation from any State, the same shall be filled in such manner as the proper authorities of the State shall direct.

Sec. 3. (1) The Congress shall be the judge of the elections, returns, and qualifications of its members; any number of deputies from a majority of the States, being present, shall constitute a quorum to do business; but a smaller number may adjourn from day to day, and may be authorized to compel the attendance of absent members; upon all questions before the Congress, each State shall be entitled to one vote, and shall be represented by any one or more of its deputies who may be present.

(2) The Congress may determine the rules of its proceedings, punish its members for disorderly behavior, and, with the concurrence of two-thirds, expel a member.

(3) The Congress shall keep a journal of its proceedings, and from time to time publish the same, excepting such parts as may in their judgment require secrecy; and the yeas and nays of the members on any question shall, at the desire of one-fifth of those present, or at the instance of any one State, be entered on the journal.

Sec. 4. The members of Congress shall receive a compensation their services, to be ascertained by law, and paid out of the Treasury of the Confederacy. They shall in all cases, except laws on the subject of treason, felony, and breach of the peace, be privileged from arrest during their attendance at the session of the Congress, and in going to and returning from the same; and for any speech or debate they shall not be questioned in any other place.

Sec. 5. (1) Every bill which shall have passed the Congress shall, before it becomes a law, be presented to the President of the Confederacy; if he approve, he shall sign it; but if not, he shall return it with his objections to the Congress, who shall enter the objections at large on their journal, and proceed to reconsider it. If, after such reconsideration, two-thirds of the Congress shall agree to pass the bill, it shall become a law. But in all such cases, the vote shall be determined by yeas and nays; and the names of the persons voting for and against the bill shall be entered on the journal. If any bill shall not be returned by the President within ten days (Sundays excepted) after it shall have been presented to him, the same shall be a law, in like manner as if he had signed it, unless the Congress, by their adjournment, prevent its return; in which case it shall not be a law. The President may veto any appropriation or appropriations and approve any other appropriation or appropriations in the same bill.

(2) Every order, resolution, or vote intended to have the force and effect of a law, shall be presented to the President, and before the same shall take effect, shall be approved by him, or, being disapproved by him, shall be repassed by two-thirds of the Congress, according to the rules and limitations prescribed in the case of a bill.

(3) Until the inauguration of the President, all bills, orders, resolutions, and votes adopted by the Congress shall be of full force without approval by him.

Sec. 6. (1) The Congress shall have power to lay and collect taxes, duties, imposts, and excises for the revenue necessary to pay the debts and carry on the Government of the Confederacy, and all duties, imposts, and excises shall be uniform throughout the States of the Confederacy.

(2) To borrow money on the credit of the Confederacy.

(3) To regulate commerce with foreign nations, and among the several States, and with the Indian tribes.

(4) To establish a uniform rule of naturalization, and uniform laws on the subject of bankruptcies throughout the Confederacy.

(5) To coin money, regulate the value thereof, and of foreign coin, and fix the standard of weights and measures.

(6) To provide for the punishment of counterfeiting the securities and current coin of the Confederacy.

(7) To establish post offices and post roads.

(8) To promote the progress of science and useful arts by securing, for limited times, to authors and inventors the exclusive right to their respective writings and discoveries.

(9) To constitute tribunals inferior to the Supreme Court.

(10) To define and punish piracies and felonies committed on the high seas, and offenses against the law of nations.

(11) To declare war, grant letters of marque and reprisal, and make rules concerning captures on land and water.

(12) To raise and support armies; but no appropriation of money to that use shall be for a longer term than two years.

(13) To provide and maintain a navy.

(14) To make rules for the government and regulation of the land and naval forces.

(15) To provide for calling forth the militia to execute the laws of the Confederacy, suppress insurrections, and repel invasions.

(16) To provide for organizing, arming, and disciplining the militia, and for governing such part of them as may be employed in the service of the Confederacy, reserving to the States respectively the appointment of the officers, and the authority of training the militia according to the discipline prescribed by Congress.

(17) To make all laws that shall be necessary and proper for carrying into execution the foregoing powers and all other powers expressly delegated by this Constitution to this Provisional Government

(18) The Congress shall have power to admit other States.

(19) This Congress shall also exercise executive powers, until the President is inaugurated.

Sec. 7. (1) The importation of African negroes from any foreign country other than the slave-holding States of the United States, is hereby forbidden; and Congress are required to pass such laws as shall effectually prevent the same.

(2) The Congress shall also have power to prohibit the introduction of slaves from any State not a member of this Confederacy.

(3) The privilege of the writ of habeas corpus shall not be suspended unless, when in cases of rebellion or invasion, the public safety may require it.

(4) No bill of attainder or ex post facto law shall be passed.

(5) No preference shall be given, by any regulation of commerce or revenue, to the ports of one State over those of another; nor shall vessels bound to or from one State be obliged to enter, clear, or pay duties in another.

(6) No money shall be drawn from the treasury, but in consequence of appropriations made by law; and a regular statement and account of the receipts and expenditures of all public money shall be published from time to time.

(7) Congress shall appropriate no money from the treasury, unless it be asked and estimated for by the President or some one of the heads of departments, except for the purpose of paying its own expenses and contingencies.

(8) No title of nobility shall be granted by the Confederacy; and no person holding any office of profit or trust under it shall, without the consent of the Congress, accept of any present, emolument, office, or title of any kind whatever, from any king, prince, or foreign state.

(9) Congress shall make no law respecting an establishment of religion, or prohibiting the free exercise thereof, or abridging the freedom of speech, or of the press; or the right of the people peaceably to assemble, and to petition the Government for a redress of such grievances as the delegated powers of this Government may warrant it to consider and redress.

(10) A well-regulated militia being necessary to the security of a free state, the right of the people to keep and bear arms shall not be infringed.

(11) No soldier shall, in time of peace, be quartered in any house without the consent of the owner; nor in time of war, but in a manner to be prescribed by law.

(12) The right of the people to be secure in their persons, houses, papers, and effects against unreasonable searches and seizures shall not be violated; and no warrants shall issue but upon probable cause, supported by oath or affirmation, and particularly describing the place to be searched, and the persons or things to be seized.

(13) No person shall be held to answer for a capital or otherwise infamous crime unless on a presentment or indictment of a grand jury, except in cases arising in the land or naval forces, or in the militia, when in actual service in time of war or public danger; nor shall any person be subject for the same offense to be twice put in jeopardy of life or limb; nor shall be compelled in any criminal case to be a witness against himself; nor be deprived of life, liberty, or property without due process of law; nor shall private property be taken for public use without just compensation.

(14) In all criminal prosecutions the accused shall enjoy the right to a speedy and public trial, by an impartial jury of the State and district wherein the crime shall have been committed, which district shall have been previously ascertained by law, and to be informed of the nature and cause of the accusation; to be confronted with the witnesses against him; to have compulsory process for obtaining witnesses in his favor; and to have the assistance of counsel for his defense.

(15) In suits at common law, where the value in controversy shall exceed twenty dollars, the right of trial by jury shall be preserved; and no fact tried by a jury shall be otherwise reexamined in any court of the Confederacy than according to the rules of the common law.

(16) Excessive bail shall not be required, nor excessive fines imposed, nor cruel and unusual punishments inflicted.

(17) The enumeration, in the Constitution, of certain rights shall not be-construed to deny or disparage others retained by the people.

(18) The powers not delegated to the Confederacy by the Constitution, nor prohibited by it to the States, are reserved to the States respectively, or to the people.

(19) The judicial power of the Confederacy shall not be construed to extend to any suit in law or equity, commenced or prosecuted against one of the States of the Confederacy, by citizens of another State, or by citizens or subjects of any foreign state.

Sec 8. (1) No State shall enter into any treaty, alliance, or confederation; grant letters of marque and reprisal; coin money; emit bills of credit; make anything but gold and silver coin a tender in payment of debts; pass any bill of attainder, ex post facto law, or law impairing the obligation of contracts; or grant any title of nobility.

(2) No State shall, without the consent of the Congress, lay any imposts or duties on imports or exports, except what may be absolutely necessary for executing its laws; and the net, produce of all duties and imposts, laid by any State on imports or exports, shall be for the use of the Treasury of the Confederacy, and all such laws shall be subject to the revision and control of the Congress. No State shall, without the consent of Congress, lay any duty of tonnage, enter into any agreement or compact with another State, or with a foreign power, or engage in war, unless actually invaded, or in such imminent danger as will not admit of delay.

ARTICLE II.

Section 1. (1) The executive power shall be vested in a President of the Confederate States of America. He, together with the Vice President, shall hold his office for one year, or until this Provisional Government shall be superseded by a permanent government, whichsoever shall first occur.

(2) The President and Vice President shall be elected by ballot by the States represented in this Congress, each State casting one vote, and a majority of the whole being requisite to elect.

(3) No person, except a natural born citizen, or a citizen of one of the States of this Confederacy at the time of the adoption of this Constitution, shall be eligible to the office of President; neither shall any person be eligible to that office who shall not have attained the age of thirty-five years, and been fourteen years a resident of one of the States of this Confederacy.

(4) In case of the removal of the President from office, or of his death, resignation, or inability to discharge the powers and duties of the said office (which inability

shall be determined by a vote of two-thirds of the Congress), the same shall devolve on the Vice President; and the Congress may by law provide for the case of removal, death, resignation, or inability, both of ths President and Vice President, declaring what officer shall then act as President; and such officer shall act accordingly until the disability be removed or a President shall be elected.

(5) The President shall at stated times receive for his services, during the period of the Provisional Government, a compensation at the rate of $25,000 per annum; and he shall not receive during that period any other emolument from this Confederacy, or any of the States thereof.

(6) Before he enter on the execution of his office he shall take the following oath or affirmation:

I do solemnly swear (or affirm) that I will faithfully execute the office of President of the Confederate States of America, and will, to the best of my ability, preserve, protect, and defend the Constitution thereof.

Sec. 2. (1) The President shall be Commander-in-Chief of the Army and Navy of the Confederacy, and of the militia of the several States, when called into the actual service of the Confederacy; he may require the opinion, in writing, of the principal officer in each of the executive departments, upon any subject relating to the duties of their respective offices; and he shall have power to grant reprieves and pardons for offenses against the Confederacy, except in eases of impeachment.

(2) He shall have power, by and with the advice and consent of the Congress, to make treaties; provided two-thirds of the Congress concur; and he shall nominate, and, by and with the advice and consent of the Congress, shall appoint ambassadors, other public ministers, and consuls, judges of the courts, and all other officers of the Confederacy whose appointments are not herein otherwise provided for, and which shall be established by law But the Congress may, by law, vest the appointment of such inferior officers as they think proper in the President alone, in the courts of law, or in the heads of departments.

(3) The President shall have power to fill up all vacancies that may happen during the recess of the Congress, by granting commissions, which shall expire at the end of their next session

Sec. 3. (1) He shall, from time to time, give to the Congress information of the state of the Confederacy, and recommend to their consideration such measures as he shall judge necessary and expedient; he may, on extraordinary occasions, convene the Congress at such times as he shall think proper; he shall receive ambassadors and other public ministers; he shall take care that the laws be faithfully executed; and shall commission all the officers of the Confederacy.

(2) The President, Vice President, and all civil officers of the Confederacy shall be removed from office on conviction by the Congress of treason, bribery, or other high crimes and misdemeanors: a vote of two-thirds shall be necessary for such conviction.

ARTICLE III

Section 1. (1) The judicial power of the Confederacy shall be vested in one Supreme Court, and in such inferior courts as are herein directed, or as the Congress may from time to time ordain and establish.

(2) Each State shall constitute a district, in which there shall be a court called a district court, which, until otherwise provided by the Congress, shall have the jurisdiction vested by the laws of the United States, as far as applicable, in both the district and circuit courts of the United States, for that State; the judge whereof shall be appointed by the President, by and with the advice and consent of the Congress, and shall, until otherwise provided by the Congress, exercise the power and authority vested by the laws of the United States in the judges of the district and circuit courts of the United States, for that State, and shall appoint the times and places at which the courts shall be held. Appeals may be taken directly from the district courts to the Supreme Court, under similar regulations to those which are provided in cases of appeal to the Supreme Court of the United States, or under such regulations as may be provided by the Congress. The commissions of all the judges shall expire with this Provisional Government. (*)

(3) The Supreme Court shall be constituted of all the district judges, a majority of whom shall be a quorum, and shall sit at such times and places as the Congress shall appoint.

(4) The Congress shall have power to make laws for the transfer of any causes which were pending in the courts of the United States, to the courts of the Confederacy, and for the execution of the orders, decrees, and judgments heretofore rendered by the said courts of the United States; and also all laws which may be requisite to protect the parties to all such suits, orders, judgments, or decrees, their heirs, personal representatives, or assignees.

Sec. 2. (1) The judicial power shall extend to all cases of law and equity, arising under this Constitution, the laws of the United States, and of this Confederacy, and treaties made, or which shall be made, under its authority; to all cases affecting ambassadors, .other public ministers, and consuls; to all cases of admiralty and maritime jurisdiction; to controversies to which the Confederacy shall be a party; controversies between two or more States; between citizens of different States; between citizens of the same State claiming lands under grants of different States.

(2) In all cases affecting ambassadors, other public ministers, and consuls, and those in which a State shall be a party, the Supreme Court shall have original jurisdiction. In all the other cases before mentioned, the Supreme Court shall have appellate jurisdiction, both as to law and fact, with such exceptions and under such regulations as the Congress shall make.

(3) The trial of all crimes, except in cases of impeachment, shall be by jury, and such trial shall be held in the State where the said crimes shall have been committed; but when not committed within any State, the trial shall be at such place or places as the Congress may by law have directed.

Sec. 3. (1) Treason against this Confederacy shall consist only in levying war against it, or in adhering to its enemies, giving them aid and comfort. No person shall be convicted of treason unless on the testimony of two witnesses to the same overt act, or on confession in open court.

(2) The Congress shall have power to declare the punishment of treason; but no attainder of treason shall work corruption of blood, or forfeiture, except during the life of the person attainted.

ARTICLE IV.

Section 1. (1) Full faith and credit shall be given in each State to the public acts, records, and judicial proceedings of every other State. And the Congress may, by general laws, prescribe the manner in which such acts, records, and proceedings shall be proved and the effect of such proof.

Sec. 2. (1) The citizens of each State shall be entitled to all privileges and immunities of citizens in the several States.

(2) A person charged in any State with treason, felony, or other crime, who shall flee from justice, and be found in another State' shall, on demand of the executive authority of the State from which he fled, be delivered up, to be removed to the State having jurisdiction of the crime.

(3) A slave in one State escaping to another, shall be delivered

up on claim of the party to whom said slave may belong by the executive authority of the State in which such slave shall be found, and in case of any abduction or forcible rescue, full compensation, including the value of the slave and all costs and expenses, shall be made to the party, by the State in which such abduction or rescue shall take place.

Sec. 3. (1) The Confederacy shall guarantee to every State in this Union a republican form of government, and shall protect each of them against invasion; and, on application of the Legislature, or of the Executive (when the Legislature cannot be convened), against domestic violence.

ARTICLE V.

I. The Congress, by a vote of two-thirds, may, at any time, alter or amend this Constitution.

ARTICLE VI.

1. This Constitution, and the laws of the Confederacy which shall be made in pursuance thereof, and all treaties made, or which shall be made, under the authority of the Confederacy, shall be the supreme law of the land; and the judges in every State shall be bound thereby, anything in the constitution or laws of any State to the contrary notwithstanding.

2. The Government hereby instituted shall take immediate steps for the settlement of all matters between the States forming it, and their other late confederates of the United States in relation to the public property and public debt at the time of their withdrawal from them; these States hereby declaring it to be their wish and earnest desire to adjust everything pertaining to the common property, common liability, and common obligations of that Union, upon the principles of right, justice, equity! and good faith.

3. Until otherwise provided by the Congress, the city of Montgomery, in the State of Alabama, shall be the seat of government.

4. The members of the Congress and all executive and judicial officers of the Confederacy shall be bound by oath or affirmation to support this Constitution; but no religious test shall be required as a qualification to any office or public trust under this Confederacy.

Done in the Congress, by the unanimous consent of all the said States, the eighth day of February, in the year of our Lord one thousand eight hundred and sixty-one, and of the Confederate States of America the first.

In witness whereof we have hereunto subscribed our names.

HOWELL COBB, President of the Congress.

South Carolina: R. Barnwell Rhett, R. W. Barnwell, James Chesnut, Jr., C. G. Memminger, William Porcher Miles, Lawrence M. Keitt, William W. Boyce, Thomas J. Withers.

Georgia: R. Toombs, Francis S. Bartow, Martin J. Crawford, E. A. Nisbet, Benjamin H. Hill, Augustus R. Wright, Thomas R. R. Cobb, A. H. Kenan, Alexander H. Stephens.

Florida: Jackson Morton, James B. Owens, J. Patton Anderson.

Alabama: Richard W. Walker, Robert H. Smith, Colin J. McRae, John Gill Shorter, William Parish Chilton, Stephen F. Hale, David P. Lewis, Thomas Fearn, J. L. M. Curry.

Mississippi: W. P. Harris, Alex. M. Clayton, W. S. Wilson, James T. Harrison, Walker Brooke, William S. Barry, J. A. P. Campbell.

Louisiana: John Perkins, Jr., Alex. de Clouet, C. M. Conrad, Duncan F. Kenner, Edward Sparrow, Henry Marshall.

By a vote of the Congress, on the 2d day of March, in the year 1861, the deputies from the State of Texas were authorized to sign the Provisional Constitution above written.

Attest. J. J. HOOPER, Secretary.

Texas: Thomas N. Waul, Williamson S. Oldham, John Gregg, John H. Reagan; W. B. Ochiltree, John Hemphill, Louis T. Wigfall.

(*) This paragraph was amended as follows:

Be it ordained by the Congress of the Confederate States of America, That the second paragraph of the first section of the third article of the Constitution of the Confederate States of America be so amended in the first line of said paragraph as to read, Each State shall, until otherwise enacted by law, constitute a district;" and in the sixth line, after the word " judge," add or judges."

Appendix D: The Constitution of the Confederate States of America (un-unannotated)

Preamble

We, the people of the Confederate States, each State acting in its sovereign and independent character, in order to form a permanent federal government, establish justice, insure domestic tranquillity, and secure the blessings of liberty to ourselves and our posterity invoking the favor and guidance of Almighty God do ordain and establish this Constitution for the Confederate States of America.

Article I

Section I. All legislative powers herein delegated shall be vested in a Congress of the Confederate States, which shall consist of a Senate and House of Representatives.

Sec. 2. (1) The House of Representatives shall be composed of members chosen every second year by the people of the several States; and the electors in each State shall be citizens of the Confederate States, and have the qualifications requisite for electors of the most numerous branch of the State Legislature; but no person of foreign birth, not a citizen of the Confederate States, shall be allowed to vote for any officer, civil or political, State or Federal.

(2) No person shall be a Representative who shall not have attained the age of twenty-five years, and be a citizen of the Confederate States, and who shall not when elected, be an inhabitant of that State in which he shall be chosen.

(3) Representatives and direct taxes shall be apportioned among the several States, which may be included within this Confederacy, according to their respective numbers, which shall be determined by adding to the whole number of free persons, including those bound to service for a term of years, and excluding Indians not taxed, three-fifths of all slaves. ,The actual enumeration shall be made within three years after the first meeting of the Congress of the Confederate States, and within every subsequent term of ten years, in such manner as they shall by law direct. The number of Representatives shall not exceed one for every fifty thousand, but each State shall have at least one Representative; and until such enumeration shall be made, the State of South Carolina shall be entitled to choose six; the State of Georgia ten; the State of Alabama nine; the State of Florida two;

the State of Mississippi seven; the State of Louisiana six; and the State of Texas six.

(4) When vacancies happen in the representation from any State the executive authority thereof shall issue writs of election to fill such vacancies.

(5) The House of Representatives shall choose their Speaker and other officers; and shall have the sole power of impeachment; except that any judicial or other Federal officer, resident and acting solely within the limits of any State, may be impeached by a vote of two-thirds of both branches of the Legislature thereof.

Sec. 3. (1) The Senate of the Confederate States shall be composed of two Senators from each State, chosen for six years by the Legislature thereof, at the regular session next immediately preceding the commencement of the term of service; and each Senator shall have one vote.

(2) Immediately after they shall be assembled, in consequence of the first election, they shall be divided as equally as may be into three classes. The seats of the Senators of the first class shall be vacated at the expiration of the second year; of the second class at the expiration of the fourth year; and of the third class at the expiration of the sixth year; so that one-third may be chosen every second year; and if vacancies happen by resignation, or other wise, during the recess of the Legislature of any State, the Executive thereof may make temporary appointments until the next meeting of the Legislature, which shall then fill such vacancies.

(3) No person shall be a Senator who shall not have attained the age of thirty years, and be a citizen of the Confederate States; and who shall not, then elected, be an inhabitant of the State for which he shall be chosen.

(4) The Vice President of the Confederate States shall be president of the Senate, but shall have no vote unless they be equally divided.

(5) The Senate shall choose their other officers; and also a president pro tempore in the absence of the Vice President, or when he shall exercise the office of President of the Confederate states.

(6) The Senate shall have the sole power to try all impeachments. When sitting for that purpose, they shall be on oath or affirmation. When the President of the Confederate States is tried, the Chief Justice shall preside; and no person shall be convicted without the concurrence of two-thirds of the members present.

(7) Judgment in cases of impeachment shall not extend further than to removal from office, and disqualification to hold any office of honor, trust, or profit under the Confederate States; but the party convicted shall, nevertheless, be liable and subject to indictment, trial, judgment, and punishment according to law.

Sec. 4. (1) The times, places, and manner of holding elections for Senators and Representatives shall be prescribed in each State by the Legislature thereof, subject to the provisions of this Constitution; but the Congress may, at any time, by law, make or alter such regulations, except as to the times and places of choosing Senators.

(2) The Congress shall assemble at least once in every year; and such meeting shall be on the first Monday in December, unless they shall, by law, appoint a different day.

Sec. 5. (1) Each House shall be the judge of the elections, returns, and qualifications of its own members, and a majority of each shall constitute a quorum to do business; but a smaller number may adjourn from day to day, and may be authorized to compel the attendance of absent members, in such manner and under such penalties as each House may provide.

(2) Each House may determine the rules of its proceedings, punish its members for disorderly behavior, and, with the concurrence of two-thirds of the whole number, expel a member.

(3) Each House shall keep a journal of its proceedings, and from time to time publish the same, excepting such parts as may in their judgment require secrecy; and the yeas and nays of the members of either House, on any question, shall, at the desire of one-fifth of those present, be entered on the journal.

(4) Neither House, during the session of Congress, shall, without the consent of the other, adjourn for more than three days, nor to any other place than that in which the two Houses shall be sitting.

Sec. 6. (1) The Senators and Representatives shall receive a compensation for their services, to be ascertained by law, and paid out of the Treasury of the Confederate States. They shall, in all cases, except treason, felony, and breach of the peace, be privileged from arrest during their attendance at the session of their respective Houses, and in going to and returning from the same; and for any speech or debate in either House, they shall not be questioned in any other place. No Senator or Representative shall, during the time for which he was elected, be appointed to any civil office under the authority of the Confederate States, which shall have been created, or the emoluments whereof shall have been increased during such time; and no person holding any office under the Confederate States shall be a member of either House during his continuance in office. But Congress may, by law, grant to the principal officer in each of the Executive Departments a seat upon the floor of either House, with the privilege of discussing any measures appertaining to his department.

Sec. 7. (1) All bills for raising revenue shall originate in the House of Representatives; but the Senate may propose or concur with amendments, as on other bills.

(2) Every bill which shall have passed both Houses, shall, before it becomes a law, be presented to the President of the Confederate States; if he approve, he shall sign it; but if not, he shall return it, with his objections, to that House in which it shall have originated, who shall enter the objections at large on their journal, and proceed to reconsider it. If, after such reconsideration, two-thirds of that House shall agree to pass the bill, it shall be sent, together with the objections, to the other House, by which it shall likewise be reconsidered, and if approved by two-thirds of that House, it shall become a law. But in all such cases, the votes of both Houses shall be determined by yeas and nays, and the names of the persons voting for and against the bill shall be entered on the journal of each House respective}y. If any bill shall not be returned by the President within ten days (Sundays excepted) after it shall have been presented to him, the same shall be a law, in like manner as if he had signed it, unless the Congress, by their adjournment, prevent its return; in which case it shall not be a law. The President may approve any appropriation and disapprove any other appropriation in the same bill. In such case he shall, in signing the bill, designate the appropriations disapproved; and shall return a copy of such appropriations, with his objections, to the House in which the bill shall have originated; and the same proceedings shall then be had as in case of other bills disapproved by the President.

(3) Every order, resolution, or vote, to which the concurrence of both Houses may be necessary (except on a question of adjournment) shall be presented to the President of the Confederate States; and before the same shall take effect, shall be approved by him; or, being disapproved by him, shall be repassed by two-thirds of both Houses, according to the rules and limitations prescribed in case of a bill.

Sec. 8. The Congress shall have power-

(1) To lay and collect taxes, duties, imposts, and excises for revenue, necessary to pay the debts, provide for the common defense, and carry on the Government of the Confederate States; but no bounties shall be granted from the Treasury; nor shall any duties or taxes on importations from foreign nations be laid to promote or foster any branch of industry; and all duties, imposts, and excises shall be uniform throughout the Confederate States.

(2) To borrow money on the credit of the Confederate States.

(3) To regulate commerce with foreign nations, and among the several States, and with the Indian tribes; but neither this, nor any other clause contained in the Constitution, shall ever be construed to delegate the power to Congress to appropriate money for any internal improvement intended to facilitate commerce; except for the purpose of furnishing lights, beacons, and buoys, and other aids to navigation upon the coasts, and the improvement of harbors and the removing of obstructions in river navigation; in all which cases such duties shall be laid on the navigation facilitated thereby as may be necessary to pay the costs and expenses thereof.

(4) To establish uniform laws of naturalization, and uniform laws on the subject of bankruptcies, throughout the Confederate States; but no law of Congress shall discharge any debt contracted before the passage of the same.

(5) To coin money, regulate the value thereof, and of foreign coin, and fix the standard of weights and measures.

(6) To provide for the punishment of counterfeiting the securities and current coin of the Confederate States.

(7) To establish post offices and post routes; but the expenses of the Post Office Department, after the Ist day of March in the year of our Lord eighteen hundred and sixty-three, shall be paid out of its own revenues.

(8) To promote the progress of science and useful arts, by securing for limited times to authors and inventors the exclusive right to their respective writings and discoveries.

(9) To constitute tribunals inferior to the Supreme Court.

(10) To define and punish piracies and felonies committed on the high seas, and offenses against the law of nations.

(11) To declare war, grant letters of marque and reprisal, and make rules concerning captures on land and water.

(12) To raise and support armies; but no appropriation of money to that use shall be for a longer term than two years.

(13) To provide and maintain a navy.

(14) To make rules for the government and regulation of the land and naval forces.

(15) To provide for calling forth the militia to execute the laws of the Confederate States, suppress insurrections, and repel invasions.

(16) To provide for organizing, arming, and disciplining the militia, and for governing such part of them as may be employed in the service of the Confederate States; reserving to the States, respectively, the appointment of the officers, and the authority of training the militia according to the discipline prescribed by Congress.

(17) To exercise exclusive legislation, in all cases whatsoever, over such district (not exceeding ten miles square) as may, by cession of one or more States and the acceptance of Congress, become the seat of the Government of the Confederate States; and to exercise like authority over all places purchased by the consent of the Legislature of the State in which the same shall be, for the erection of forts, magazines, arsenals, dockyards, and other needful buildings; and

(18) To make all laws which shall be necessary and proper for carrying into execution the foregoing powers, and all other powers vested by this Constitution in the Government of the Confederate States, or in any department or officer thereof.

Sec. 9. (1) The importation of negroes of the African race from any foreign country other than the slaveholding States or Territories of the United States of America, is hereby forbidden; and Congress is required to pass such laws as shall effectually prevent the same.

(2) Congress shall also have power to prohibit the introduction of slaves from any State not a member of, or Territory not belonging to, this Confederacy.

(3) The privilege of the writ of habeas corpus shall not be suspended, unless when in cases of rebellion or invasion the public safety may require it.

(4) No bill of attainder, ex post facto law, or law denying or impairing the right of property in negro slaves shall be passed.

(5) No capitation or other direct tax shall be laid, unless in proportion to the census or enumeration hereinbefore directed to be taken.

(6) No tax or duty shall be laid on articles exported from any State, except by a vote of two-thirds of both Houses.

(7) No preference shall be given by any regulation of commerce or revenue to the ports of one State over those of another.

(8) No money shall be drawn from the Treasury, but in consequence of appropriations made by law; and a regular statement and account of the receipts and expenditures of all public money shall be published from time to time.

(9) Congress shall appropriate no money from the Treasury except by a vote of two-thirds of both Houses, taken by yeas and nays, unless it be asked and estimated for by some one of the heads of departments and submitted to Congress by the President; or for the purpose of paying its own expenses and contingencies; or for the payment of claims against the Confederate States, the justice of which shall have been judicially declared by a tribunal for the investigation of claims against the Government, which it is hereby made the duty of Congress to establish.

(10) All bills appropriating money shall specify in Federal currency the exact amount of each appropriation and the purposes for which it is made; and Congress shall grant no extra compensation to any public contractor, officer, agent, or servant, after such contract shall have been made or such service rendered.

(11) No title of nobility shall be granted by the Confederate States; and no person holding any office of profit or trust under them shall, without the consent of the Congress, accept of any present, emolument, office, or title of any kind whatever, from any king, prince, or foreign state.

(12) Congress shall make no law respecting an establishment of religion, or prohibiting the free exercise thereof; or abridging the freedom of speech, or of the

press; or the right of the people peaceably to assemble and petition the Government for a redress of grievances.

(13) A well-regulated militia being necessary to the security of a free State, the right of the people to keep and bear arms shall not be infringed.

(14) No soldier shall, in time of peace, be quartered in any house without the consent of the owner; nor in time of war, but in a manner to be prescribed by law.

(15) The right of the people to be secure in their persons, houses, papers, and effects, against unreasonable searches and seizures, shall not be violated; and no warrants shall issue but upon probable cause, supported by oath or affirmation, and particularly describing the place to be searched and the persons or things to be seized.

(16) No person shall be held to answer for a capital or otherwise infamous crime, unless on a presentment or indictment of a grand jury, except in cases arising in the land or naval forces, or in the militia, when in actual service in time of war or public danger; nor shall any person be subject for the same offense to be twice put in jeopardy of life or limb; nor be compelled, in any criminal case, to be a witness against himself; nor be deprived of life, liberty, or property without due process of law; nor shall private property be taken for public use, without just compensation.

(17) In all criminal prosecutions the accused shall enjoy the right to a speedy and public trial, by an impartial jury of the State and district wherein the crime shall have been committed, which district shall have been previously ascertained by law, and to be informed of the nature and cause of the accusation; to be confronted with the witnesses against him; to have compulsory process for obtaining witnesses in his favor; and to have the assistance of counsel for his defense.

(18) In suits at common law, where the value in controversy shall exceed twenty dollars, the right of trial by jury shall be preserved; and no fact so tried by a jury shall be otherwise reexamined in any court of the Confederacy, than according to the rules of common law.

(19) Excessive bail shall not be required, nor excessive fines imposed, nor cruel and unusual punishments inflicted.

(20) Every law, or resolution having the force of law, shall relate to but one subject, and that shall be expressed in the title.

Sec. 10. (1) No State shall enter into any treaty, alliance, or confederation; grant letters of marque and reprisal; coin money; make anything but gold and silver coin a tender in payment of debts; pass any bill of attainder, or ex post facto law, or law impairing the obligation of contracts; or grant any title of nobility.

(2) No State shall, without the consent of the Congress, lay any imposts or duties on imports or exports, except what may be absolutely necessary for executing its inspection laws; and the net produce of all duties and imposts, laid by any State on imports, or exports, shall be for the use of the Treasury of the Confederate States; and all such laws shall be subject to the revision and control of Congress.

(3) No State shall, without the consent of Congress, lay any duty on tonnage, except on seagoing vessels, for the improvement of its rivers and harbors navigated by the said vessels; but such duties shall not conflict with any treaties of the Confederate States with foreign nations; and any surplus revenue thus derived shall, after making such improvement, be paid into the common treasury. Nor shall any State keep troops or ships of war in time of peace, enter into any agreement or compact with another State, or with a foreign power, or engage in war, unless actually invaded, or in such imminent danger as will not admit of delay. But when any river divides or flows through two or more States they may enter into compacts with each other to improve the navigation thereof.

ARTICLE II

Section I. (1) The executive power shall be vested in a President of the Confederate States of America. He and the Vice President shall hold their offices for the term of six years; but the President shall not be reeligible. The President and Vice President shall be elected as follows:

(2) Each State shall appoint, in such manner as the Legislature thereof may direct, a number of electors equal to the whole number of Senators and Representatives to which the State may be entitled in the Congress; but no Senator or Representative or person holding an office of trust or profit under the Confederate States shall be appointed an elector.

(3) The electors shall meet in their respective States and vote by ballot for President and Vice President, one of whom, at least, shall not be an inhabitant of the same State with themselves; they shall name in their ballots the person voted for as President, and in distinct ballots the person voted for as Vice President, and

they shall make distinct lists of all persons voted for as President, and of all persons voted for as Vice President, and of the number of votes for each, which lists they shall sign and certify, and transmit, sealed, to the seat of the Government of. the Confederate States, directed to the President of the Senate; the President of the Senate shall, in the presence of the Senate and House of Representatives, open all the certificates, and the votes shall then be counted; the person having the greatest number of votes for President shall be the President, if such number be a majority of the whole number of electors appointed; and if no person have such majority, then from the persons having the highest numbers, not exceeding three, on the list of those voted for as President, the House of Representatives shall choose immediately, by ballot, the President. But in choosing the President the votes shall be taken by States, the representation from each State having one vote; a quorum for this purpose shall consist of a member or members from two-thirds of the States, and a majority of all the States shall be necessary to a choice. And if the House of Representatives shall not choose a President, whenever the right of choice shall devolve upon them, before the 4th day of March next following, then the Vice President shall act as President, as in case of the death, or other constitutional disability of the President.

(4) The person having the greatest number of votes as Vice President shall be the Vice President, if such number be a majority of the whole number of electors appointed; and if no person have a majority, then, from the two highest numbers on the list, the Senate shall choose the Vice President; a quorum for the purpose shall consist of two-thirds of the whole number of Senators, and a majority of the whole number shall be necessary to a choice.

(5) But no person constitutionally ineligible to the office of President shall be eligible to that of Vice President of the Confederate States.

(6) The Congress may determine the time of choosing the electors, and the day on which they shall give their votes; which day shall be the same throughout the Confederate States.

(7) No person except a natural-born citizen of the Confederate; States, or a citizen thereof at the time of the adoption of this Constitution, or a citizen thereof born in the United States prior to the 20th of December, 1860, shall be eligible to the office of President; neither shall any person be eligible to that office who shall not have attained the age of thirty-five years, and been fourteen years a resident within the limits of the Confederate States, as they may exist at the time of his election.

(8) In case of the removal of the President from office, or of his death, resignation, or inability to discharge the powers and duties of said office, the same shall devolve on the Vice President; and the Congress may, by law, provide for the case of removal, death, resignation, or inability, both of the President and Vice President, declaring what officer shall then act as President; and such officer shall act accordingly until the disability be removed or a President shall be elected.

(9) The President shall, at stated times, receive for his services a compensation, which shall neither be increased nor diminished during the period for which he shall have been elected; and he shall not receive within that period any other emolument from the Confederate States, or any of them.

(10) Before he enters on the execution of his office he shall take the following oath or affirmation: "I do solemnly swear (or affirm) that I will faithfully execute the office of President of the Confederate States, and will, to the best of my ability, preserve, protect, and defend the Constitution thereof.

Sec. 2. (1) The President shall be Commander-in-Chief of the Army and Navy of the Confederate States, and of the militia of the several States, when called into the actual service of the Confederate States; he may require the opinion, in writing, of the principal officer in each of the Executive Departments, upon any subject relating to the duties of their respective offices; and he shall have power to grant reprieves and pardons for offenses against the Confederate States, except in cases of impeachment.

(2) He shall have power, by and with the advice and consent of the Senate, to make treaties; provided two-thirds of the Senators present concur; and he shall nominate, and by and with the advice and consent of the Senate shall appoint, ambassadors, other public ministers and consuls, judges of the Supreme Court, and all other officers of the Confederate States whose appointments are not herein otherwise provided for, and which shall be established by law; but the Congress may, by law, vest the appointment of such inferior officers, as they think proper, in the President alone, in the courts of law, or in the heads of departments.

(3) The principal officer in each of the Executive Departments, and all persons connected with the diplomatic service, may be removed from office at the pleasure of the President. All other civil officers of the Executive Departments may be removed at any time by the President, or other appointing power, when their services are unnecessary, or for dishonesty, incapacity, inefficiency, misconduct,

or neglect of duty; and when so removed, the removal shall be reported to the Senate, together with the reasons therefor.

(4) The President shall have power to fill all vacancies that may happen during the recess of the Senate, by granting commissions which shall expire at the end of their next session; but no person rejected by the Senate shall be reappointed to the same office during their ensuing recess.

Sec. 3. (1) The President shall, from time to time, give to the Congress information of the state of the Confederacy, and recommend to their consideration such measures as he shall judge necessary and expedient; he may, on extraordinary occasions, convene both Houses, or either of them; and in case of disagreement between them, with respect to the time of adjournment, he may adjourn them to such time as he shall think proper; he shall receive ambassadors and other public ministers; he shall take care that the laws be faithfully executed, and shall commission all the officers of the Confederate States.

Sec. 4. (1) The President, Vice President, and all civil officers of the Confederate States, shall be removed from office on impeachment for and conviction of treason, bribery, or other high crimes and misdemeanors.

ARTICLE III

Section I. (1) The judicial power of the Confederate States shall be vested in one Supreme Court, and in such inferior courts as the Congress may, from time to time, ordain and establish. The judges, both of the Supreme and inferior courts, shall hold their offices during good behavior, and shall, at stated times, receive for their services a compensation which shall not be diminished during their continuance in office.

Sec. 2. (1) The judicial power shall extend to all cases arising under this Constitution, the laws of the Confederate States, and treaties made, or which shall be made, under their authority; to all cases affecting ambassadors, other public ministers and consuls; to all cases of admiralty and maritime jurisdiction; to controversies to which the Confederate States shall be a party; to controversies between two or more States; between a State and citizens of another State, where the State is plaintiff; between citizens claiming lands under grants of different States; and between a State or the citizens thereof, and foreign states, citizens, or subjects; but no State shall be sued by a citizen or subject of any foreign state.

(2) In all cases affecting ambassadors, other public ministers and consuls, and those in which a State shall be a party, the Supreme Court shall have original jurisdiction. In all the other cases before mentioned, the Supreme Court shall have appellate jurisdiction both as to law and fact, with such exceptions and under such regulations as the Congress shall make.

(3) The trial of all crimes, except in cases of impeachment, shall be by jury, and such trial shall be held in the State where the said crimes shall have been committed; but when not committed within any State, the trial shall be at such place or places as the Congress may by law have directed.

Sec. 3. (1) Treason against the Confederate States shall consist only in levying war against them, or in adhering to their enemies, giving them aid and comfort. No person shall be convicted of treason unless on the testimony of two witnesses to the same overt act, or on confession in open court.

(2) The Congress shall have power to declare the punishment of treason; but no attainder of treason shall work corruption of blood, or forfeiture, except during the life of the person attainted.

ARTICLE IV

Section I. (1) Full faith and credit shall be given in each State to the public acts, records, and judicial proceedings of every other State; and the Congress may, by general laws, prescribe the manner in which such acts, records, and proceedings shall be proved, and the effect thereof.

Sec. 2. (1) The citizens of each State shall be entitled to all the privileges and immunities of citizens in the several States; and shall have the right of transit and sojourn in any State of this Confederacy, with their slaves and other property; and the right of property in said slaves shall not be thereby impaired.

(2) A person charged in any State with treason, felony, or other crime against the laws of such State, who shall flee from justice, and be found in another State, shall, on demand of the executive authority of the State from which he fled, be delivered up, to be removed to the State having jurisdiction of the crime.

(3) No slave or other person held to service or labor in any State or Territory of the Confederate States, under the laws thereof, escaping or lawfully carried into another, shall, in consequence of any law or regulation therein, be discharged from

such service or labor; but shall be delivered up on claim of the party to whom such slave belongs,. or to whom such service or labor may be due.

Sec. 3. (1) Other States may be admitted into this Confederacy by a vote of two-thirds of the whole House of Representatives and two-thirds of the Senate, the Senate voting by States; but no new State shall be formed or erected within the jurisdiction of any other State, nor any State be formed by the junction of two or more States, or parts of States, without the consent of the Legislatures of the States concerned, as well as of the Congress.

(2) The Congress shall have power to dispose of and make all needful rules and regulations concerning the property of the Confederate States, including the lands thereof.

(3) The Confederate States may acquire new territory; and Congress shall have power to legislate and provide governments for the inhabitants of all territory belonging to the Confederate States, lying without the limits of the several Sates; and may permit them, at such times, and in such manner as it may by law provide, to form States to be admitted into the Confederacy. In all such territory the institution of negro slavery, as it now exists in the Confederate States, shall be recognized and protected be Congress and by the Territorial government; and the inhabitants of the several Confederate States and Territories shall have the right to take to such Territory any slaves lawfully held by them in any of the States or Territories of the Confederate States.

(4) The Confederate States shall guarantee to every State that now is, or hereafter may become, a member of this Confederacy, a republican form of government; and shall protect each of them against invasion; and on application of the Legislature or of the Executive when the Legislature is not in session) against domestic violence.

ARTICLE V

Section I. (1) Upon the demand of any three States, legally assembled in their several conventions, the Congress shall summon a convention of all the States, to take into consideration such amendments to the Constitution as the said States shall concur in suggesting at the time when the said demand is made; and should any of the proposed amendments to the Constitution be agreed on by the said convention, voting by States, and the same be ratified by the Legislatures of two- thirds of the several States, or by conventions in two-thirds thereof, as the one or the other mode of ratification may be proposed by the general convention, they shall

thenceforward form a part of this Constitution. But no State shall, without its consent, be deprived of its equal representation in the Senate.

ARTICLE VI

I. The Government established by this Constitution is the successor of the Provisional Government of the Confederate States of America, and all the laws passed by the latter shall continue in force until the same shall be repealed or modified; and all the officers appointed by the same shall remain in office until their successors are appointed and qualified, or the offices abolished.

2. All debts contracted and engagements entered into before the adoption of this Constitution shall be as valid against the Confederate States under this Constitution, as under the Provisional Government.

3. This Constitution, and the laws of the Confederate States made in pursuance thereof, and all treaties made, or which shall be made, under the authority of the Confederate States, shall be the supreme law of the land; and the judges in every State shall be bound thereby, anything in the constitution or laws of any State to the contrary notwithstanding.

4. The Senators and Representatives before mentioned, and the members of the several State Legislatures, and all executive and judicial officers, both of the Confederate States and of the several States, shall be bound by oath or affirmation to support this Constitution; but no religious test shall ever be required as a qualification to any office or public trust under the Confederate States.

5. The enumeration, in the Constitution, of certain rights shall not be construed to deny or disparage others retained by the people of the several States.

6. The powers not delegated to the Confederate States by the Constitution, nor prohibited by it to the States, are reserved to the States, respectively, or to the people thereof.

ARTICLE VII

I. The ratification of the conventions of five States shall be sufficient for the establishment of this Constitution between the States so ratifying the same.

2. When five States shall have ratified this Constitution, in the manner before specified, the Congress under the Provisional Constitution shall prescribe the time for holding the election of President and Vice President; and for the meeting of the Electoral College; and for counting the votes, and inaugurating the President. They shall, also, prescribe the time for holding the first election of members of Congress under this Constitution, and the time for assembling the same. Until the assembling of such Congress, the Congress under the Provisional Constitution shall continue to exercise the legislative powers granted them; not extending beyond the time limited by the Constitution of the Provisional Government.

Adopted unanimously by the Congress of the Confederate States of South Carolina, Georgia, Florida, Alabama, Mississippi, Louisiana, and Texas, sitting in convention at the capitol, the city of Montgomery, Ala., on the eleventh day of March, in the year eighteen hundred and Sixty-one.

HOWELL COBB, President of the Congress.

South Carolina: R. Barnwell Rhett, C. G. Memminger, Wm. Porcher Miles, James Chesnut, Jr., R. W. Barnwell, William W. Boyce, Lawrence M. Keitt, T. J. Withers.

Georgia: Francis S. Bartow, Martin J. Crawford, Benjamin H. Hill, Thos. R. R. Cobb.

Florida: Jackson Morton, J. Patton Anderson, Jas. B. Owens.

Alabama: Richard W. Walker, Robt. H. Smith, Colin J. McRae, William P. Chilton, Stephen F. Hale, David P. Lewis, Tho. Fearn, Jno. Gill Shorter, J. L. M. Curry.

Mississippi: Alex. M. Clayton, James T. Harrison, William S. Barry, W. S. Wilson, Walker Brooke, W. P. Harris, J. A. P. Campbell.

Louisiana: Alex. de Clouet, C. M. Conrad, Duncan F. Kenner, Henry Marshall.

Texas: John Hemphill, Thomas N. Waul, John H. Reagan, Williamson S. Oldham, Louis T. Wigfall, John Gregg, William Beck Ochiltree.

About the Author

Sean Kevin Gravel was born in Pensacola, Florida. Growing up there he achieved the rank of Eagle Scout and later attended the University of West Florida, earning a Bachelor of Arts degree in History with a Pre-Law Specialization. He then attended law school at Florida State University, earning his Juris Doctorate in 2015 and was admitted to the Florida Bar later that year. He currently lives in Daytona Beach, Florida with his wife Lindsay and practices criminal appellate law. He is also the author of *The History of the Confederate States of America: How Things Would Have Been Different Had the South Won.*